MYSTICAL PASSION
Spirituality for a Bored Society

MYSTICAL PASSION
Spirituality for a Bored Society

by

William McNamara, O.C.D.

PAULIST PRESS
New York/Ramsey/Toronto

Library of Congress
Catalog Card Number: 77-80801

ISBN: 0-8091-2053-4

Published by Paulist Press
Editorial Office: 1865 Broadway, New York, N.Y. 10023
Business Office: 545 Island Road, Ramsey, N.J. 07446

Printed and bound in the
United States of America

ACKNOWLEDGMENTS

We wish to express our gratitude to the publishers and copyright owners cited here for their permission to quote from the following works:

THE COMPLETE WORKS OF SWAMI VIVEKANANDA by Swami Vivekananda. Mayavati, Advaita Ashrama, 1955. Reprinted with permission.

CONTEMPLATION IN A WORLD OF ACTION by Thomas Merton. Copyright © 1965, 1969, 1970, 1971 by the Trustees of the Merton Legacy Trust. Reprinted by permission of Doubleday & Co., Inc.

"The Decade of the Great Liberal Death Wish" by Malcolm Muggeridge. Copyright © 1970 by Malcolm Muggeridge. First published in ESQUIRE MAGAZINE. Reprinted by permission of Harold Ober Associates Inc.

DISPUTED QUESTIONS by Thomas Merton. New York, Farrar, Straus & Cudahy, 1953. Reprinted by permission of the copyright owner.

JOAN OF ARC by Hilaire Belloc. New York, Declan & McMullen Co., 1949.

LETTERS AND PAPERS FROM PRISON by Dietrich Bonhoeffer. Edited by E. Bethge, trans. by R. Fuller. New York, The Macmillan Co., 1962. Reprinted by permission of the copyright owner.

THE LETTERS OF EVELYN UNDERHILL ed. by Charles Williams. London, Longmans, Green, 1943.

LOVE AND WILL by Rollo May. New York, W. W. Norton & Co., 1969. Reprinted by permission of the copyright owner.

Contents

Yahweh proclaims himself *El Kana*, a passionate God, panting
in hot pursuit of man whom he loves.

God's steadfast love is his *hesed*, his pledged passion. Sacred
history is the turbulent and tumultuous record of love between
God and his people.

Revelation is the irruption of divine passion in the human
domain. In his entire lifetime of passion, Christ suffered the
onslaughts of divine love and the exigencies of human becoming. Breaking out of the confines of the world's sheep pen, he
discovered that he could roar like a lion, not bleat like a lamb.

God who is love is certainly not static but infinitely dynamic.
He is the most moved Mover as well as the unmoved Mover.
He is no self-sufficient autocratic potentate ruling the world in-
differently from above, independent of man. God himself suf-
fers in the burning at Buchenwald, the bleeding in Southeast
Asia, and the starving in Bangladesh.

The passion of God meets and evokes the passion of man and
through this com-passion, the hard crust of the world is broken
open. Within the Christian tradition the word passion takes on
a very distinctive meaning. Powerful passion creates the
mighty dynamic strength of the colossal saints.

St. Paul was not knocked off his high horse by the God of universal amiability but the supra-personal, possessive God of
Israel, demanding a concrete channelling of Paul's love into a
passionate and definite relationship with jealously guarded
boundaries. Precisely because Paul is such a great lover, there
are things that he hates. In his letters there is a fundamental
and necessary complementarity of love and wrath.

Elizabeth of Hungary was sanctified because all her natural
human stuff was raised to the limit. Her spiritual life was a
vibrantly rich emotional life. She did not find the love of God
incompatible with a real, natural, burning love of a human

being. She pleasured her husband like any playfully saucy wife, cared for the poor like a 13th-century Mother Teresa, and begged God to squander whatever passion remained unspent in her.

Joan of Arc took the world seriously. She did not flee the arena to remain untainted or renounce the world to be protected from it. She became a thoroughly humanized saint according to her own inner truth: by riding horses, crowning kings, and being burned at the stake. Life itself was her asceticism. She was willing to suffer whatever it required of her.

Therese of Lisieux shows us that the recovery of childhood is the condition of discipleship and of human maturity. The spirituality of childhood which dominates the Christian tradition requires no strongman acts, no glittering achievements, no spectacular successes, nothing big or dramatic at all, but a passionate fidelity to a hundred little things.

The higher experiences of the spiritual life are most desirable. But they are most likely to occur if we are at home with the daily things that fill our lives. The inner truths of these good things are always accessible. If we stay in touch and remain faithful to them, we will be ready when He comes. But in this age of immense sophistication, the perceptive appreciation of the secret surprise of customary objects is a very rare and precious kind of experience, enjoyed almost exclusively by unspoiled children, undistinguished sages, and unemployed clowns.

Our central malaise is not the obvious evil in the streets but the subtle and surreptitious corrosion of "pretty poison," the great passion killer. Two examples of pretty poison are:

We will understand ourselves only if we come to fathom our own language. Pretty poison gradually kills the spirit of a nation by the corrosion of its language. The deplorable impoverishment of our language and our love is celebrated by Erich Segal and Erica Jong. An OK love story is no love story at all.

Catholic Pentecostalism is not an appropriate response to divine passion but a diversionary tactic that teaches us how to get close enough to God to be warmed by him without being burned by his consuming fire. We must be sure to pray but slow to pray, God-conscious and not prayer-conscious. We need to keep our eyes on Christ and follow the pattern of the big saints, seeking only the miracle of *metanoia*.

The constant in all forms of pretty poison is paltriness, the opposite of passion. We are over-developed, over-civilized, and over-protected. We need wild things and wilderness places to ready us for the absolutely unmitigated wildness of God.

The desert is an antidote to pretty poison. It is not a natural phenomenon but a way of life.

The desert experience cannot take any random form. It must break the pattern of our ordinary existence, destroy mediocrity, distinguish between the vital and moribund. The desert is an invitation to a contest, a confrontation with the real, a proclamation of God's absolute sovereignty.

The prophets Moses, Elijah, and Hosea show us that the desert is the "place" where God visits his people, leading them through purgation into paradise.

The desert continues to be experienced in the lives of John the Baptist, Paul, the Desert Fathers, and Jesus himself, whose *decisive* cosmic struggle took place in the wilderness.

When the physical desert is inaccessible, the desert may be experienced through the silence and solitude of a retreat, tough and towering monastic life, a robust and rugged lenten season, and the Spiritual Life Institute.

Our plight today is similar to the enslaved condition of the Jews in Egypt prior to their liberating desert experience.

We have become inextricably entangled in the life of the flesh. The "flesh" does not refer to bodily life, but to mundane life, our external and public self, based on human respect or social preoccupation, which smothers the life of the spirit.

Passion breaks through the tight teguments of the flesh and paves the way for the transformation of the raw matter of our lives by the power of the spirit. Passion is the power that drives men toward God whom we all must ultimately choose. It requires a compelling imaginative symbol on which to focus its energy. Passion must be enlightened by reason and reason must be kindled by passion.

The untamed evil urges in us are natural but must be recognized, affirmed, and incorporated into the personality or our spiritual lives suffer terrible deprivation. Repressed daemonic elements assert themselves revengefully in aggression and violence such as in *The Exorcist*.

We are afraid of passion because it leads us beyond the carefully measured boundaries of the conscious self. We disguise our fear of life as well as death in our compulsive pursuit of happiness. Thrashing in and out of war and each other's beds, we pursue the shadow of our happiness, succumbing to hypocrisy, the greatest sin against the spirit, ending up passionless or a-pathetic.

Eros is the Greek word for passion. We have exchanged the wild and wonderful passion of eros for the tame and timid sensation of sex, ekeing out a quasi-existence on vicarious venereal pleasures. Afraid of the driving force of eros, we have nothing left to celebrate but genital technique. When there is no eros at the creative center of a culture, the degradation of man and the collapse of his civilization is assured.

There is no love without tragecy. Erotic love hurls us into simultaneous heights and depths. Love-force is a tragic gift. To keep our love alive we must be in continual creative relation to the symbol and source of our passion as we move in fidelity from romantic love to mystical love.

TO
TESSA

Passion

Passion between the covers
of a book
    May come in the form of
the undraped body of
    Anybody's whore
    Or the naked form of
a man hanging from a
    Crossarmed tree
disarmingly unarmed,
    Save for the look of love.*

---

*Sherwood A. Treadwell, *The Christian Century*, Dec. 30, 1970, p. 1554.

Preface

My main purpose is to offer as definite and clear an idea as possible of the meaning, function, and end of passion; and then convince the reader to go ahead and live passionately.

And forever. That's the distinctively human trait—it goes on and on. That's why it is always appropriate to say to a human: "Be yourself," because becoming himself is an ongoing, unending task. This would be a senseless thing to say to a rhinoceros since a rhino has already achieved the quintessence of rhinocerocity.

Human destiny is, in a sense, endless, precisely because it is an exploration into God. The false and fixating sense of "having arrived" or "having finished" is one of the most dehumanizing attitudes of which we are capable. We must be always on the move, always beginning: all over again but into realms of which we are not yet conscious, into Love beyond all our other loves. Our passion must always be mounting.

Mount of Passion is eros becoming agape. Anders Nygren's dichotomy between these two loves in an otherwise outstanding book, *Agape and Eros*, must be rejected. The anti-eros conclusions reached by Denis de Rougemont in *Love in the Western World* were eventually corrected in *Love Declared*, a subsequent work by the same celebrated author. Both de Rougemont books are well worth reading. But by far the best work on the subject of eros and agape is *The Mind and Heart of Love* by Martin D'Arcy who recognizes that these two basic human forces must always be united in an indissoluble bond. It is encouraging to see a contemporary psychiatrist as reliable and renowned as Rollo May reemphasizing the wedding of eros and agape in such a practical and irrefutable way as he does so splendidly in his *Love and Will*.

Pious platitudes about eros and agape are not convincing. Neither is merely abstract thinking. A positive definition and delineation of passion in all its glory makes a certain kind of con-

1

tribution, but an unbalanced one. If I am trying to convince my readers to live passionately, it is not enough for me to establish the pure origins of passion in God, the authentic tradition of passion in the Church, and the dire need for passion in the world today. I must also point out, if I am to be true to myself and a reliable guide to my readers, whether or not contemporary movements, modes, and models of passion are helpful.

This book is not merely an individual effort. It could not have been done without the helpful work of my community at Nova Nada, Nova Scotia and the passion of my community-at-large.

I hope that ample personal communion is achieved and enough self-revelation occurs to make this an existential account. A book on passion certainly ought to convey some of the author's own emotions. Yet this book is not as specific as I intended it to be. Another book, far more explicit, will have to be written, in answer to the many questions raised here.

1: Mystical Passion

Married lovers are not sexual and passionate enough. And what's more, neither are celibate lovers, who should be at least as sexual and passionate as married people. There is no other way to be a really great lover. And if religious men and women are not great lovers, what hope is there for Christianity?

I stake the future on the few humble and hearty lovers who seek God passionately in the marvelous, messy world of redeemed and related realities that lie in front of our noses. These lovers may not be legion, but there is a sufficient number to reveal a Christlike way for married men and women to have intimate friends and for celibates to have chaste relationships that are obviously and joyously forms of appropriate interactions between highly sexed persons. I have met just enough of such happy, wholesome personalities to make me suitably optimistic to presume that the progress of Teilhard de Chardin's noosphere and the emotional maturation of mankind are in the process of being accomplished with such rapidity that an increasingly greater number of men and women benefit by such relationships. All we hear about are the failures and ridiculous solutions: spouse swapping, comarital sex, open marriage, divorce, marriage for priests and sisters, or "the third way" reported in *Newsweek*.[1]

Recent books on sexuality and intimacy by such good men as Andrew Greeley and Eugene Kennedy have been long overdue. They have been an immense help to many. But there is an even greater need right now, an absolutely indispensable need for living witnesses: not for people who erroneously think they have solved the problem, or who arrogantly claim to have reached perfection, but for followers of Christ who become progressively

---

1. "Priests Who Date: 'The Third Way,'" *Newsweek*, Dec. 3, 1973, pp. 107-110 B.

conscious of a human growth that is as thoroughly erotic and sexual as it is spiritual.

None of us is unaffected by the accumulation of human diminishments, the mystery of iniquity, the ravages of sin. Except for the mercy of God, I myself would be in desperate straits over the degree to which I feel the crunch of evil. Crippled by sin, my life is healed by the touch of God. But the healing of God is also unhinging. It seems to involve me in paradoxes. I am commited to solitude, but am called to preach and to teach. I am drawn into silence, but am compelled to write. I am a marked man, seared by the consuming fire of God's love, by the total ravishments of his exclusive, possessive, summons; and yet I am always falling in love with feeble, finite creatures, and rightly so. I am conscious of divine prodigy and human impotence, of divine pathos and human apathy, of God's fidelity and man's idolatry, of God's beingfulness and my nothingness.

The Courage to Burn

How distressing that the divine fury has not yet devoured me! Sacerdotal longevity worries me. It makes me suspect that I have not lived passionately enough, that I have merely warmed myself by the fire that Christ came into the world to ignite, but have not been consumed by it. It seems to me that the fierce and fiery men of God don't last long: they burn out quickly.

I think of the young novice in the desert who went to the elder, the holy man of God, and said: "Father, according as I am able, I keep my little Rule, and my little fast, my prayer, meditation, and contemplative silence; and according as I am able, I strive to cleanse my heart of thoughts. Now, what more should I do?" The elder rose up in reply and stretched out his hands to heaven, and his fingers became like ten lamps of fire. He said: "Why not be totally changed into fire?"

Few of us have the courage to burn—to be totally called, awesomely marked, thoroughly spent, and imperiously sent. The divine summons is ignored, the human vocation is dodged, and the eternal banquet, celebrating the final love affair, is postponed because we are so fearful. Ignorance and fear have plagued us from the beginning until now and are responsible for our multiple idolatries.

The masses are offended by the few who will not perish with them, who will not be driven like cattle into the latest, greenest, most modern cow palace or sheep pen. We are witnessing today an oceanic upheaval of values. Multitudes are drowning. Humankind has reached such despair in the wake of recent worldwide disillusionment that millions are willing to drown if only all will go down in euphoric togetherness. The few who are learning to swim in order to save are bitterly resented. They must have no firm ground of their own on which to stand in contemplative faith and spousal love, but must get swallowed up like the rest of devastated mankind in intellectual absurdity, disguised despair, and the barren business of middle-class America.

This condition of the people, at once sophisticated and dehumanized, forces the majority to ask the wrong questions to which there are no right answers. The preface to *The Human Adventure* bears repeating as an example. Our apostolic hermits in the woods of Nova Scotia and the desert of Arizona are always being asked to justify their simple and solitary existence, although their way of life is one of the few genuinely human styles in North America. In addition, they offer their fellowmen, religious or not, Christian or not, a human climate in which they may learn to breathe and live and love again. The right question is the one the woodsmen and desertmen should ask the madding crowd: is it possible to justify a complicated and crowded life, in ugly surroundings, in slavery to Mammon, in a vacuum of love, in defiance of God?[2]

There is, of course, no justification. There can only be a confession of guilt.

What's wrong with the world? What's wrong with the nation, the community, the Church? What's wrong with youth, with parents? What's wrong with the schools? What's wrong with our economy, our politics, our cultural and religious life?

These are the questions heard round the world. They are

---

2. This question is not rhetorical, for in *Desert Call*, published quarterly by the Spiritual Life Institute, Sedona, Arizona, we have initiated an on-going dialogue on "Contemplation in the City," which is eliciting articulate and creative responses from metropolitan and suburban areas all over the country.

questions that must be answered whatever the cost. Until we
come up with some satisfactory answers, we will perpetuate our
present quandary: a perfectly ironic and equal coincidence between
technological progress and human suffering.

But there will be no satisfactory answer until the questions
are changed. Let me ask the right question: what's wrong with
me? This question is not a private question since I am not a private
person.

"No man is an island," the solitary least of all. Besides,
what's wrong with me is what's wrong, more or less, with everyone. And the varying degrees and forms of what is essentially
wrong with me and everyone else are what is essentially wrong
with the world.

I know what's wrong with me: I am not passionate enough.
I am not being aroused and lured into the sheer totality of me,
which God desires with infinite desire to fashion out of the undreamed of and undeveloped potentialities of my being; and which
Jesus has claimed and demonstrated to be not only realizable but
imperative. I am not completely in tune with the universe, with
the universality of being, with Being itself. If I am alienated, frustrated, and lonely, it is because I am out of touch with the center
of things. If I am out of touch with the center of things, with God,
it is because I do not take God with unconditional seriousness;
that is to say, I do not allow myself to be ruled and governed by
one, pure passion.

The life of any person of outstanding quality is borne forward
on the wings of a great passion. This is also true of a family, a
religious or civic community, and of the nation. Modern civilization has lost so much strength and power because of its remarkably low level of affectivity, particularly of passion. There is even
something about the new life-style of youth that is listless and
lackadaisical. Every time I read a newspaper or a magazine, every
time I go onto a college campus or into a coffee shop or a typical
downtown office, every time I hear confessions or go to church, see
a movie or watch television, visit friends or even examine my own
conscience, I come to the same conclusion: what we all desperately
need in gargantuan measures is an irrepressible zest for life,
with an overruling, specific, personal, and passionate objective.
This objective need not be pellucidly clear and it may, undoubtedly
should, change its form as we go on putting one foot in front of the

other. En route, illusions, disappointments, contradictions should be expected, overcome, and transcended. We need to integrate all contradictory elements into a higher synthesis, but this is possible only through a total commitment and surrender to something greater than all these contradictions. It takes a humorous and stubborn man to overcome the inevitable obstacles from within and without.

It took me ten years to begin to achieve what I set out to do with the Spiritual Life Institute in 1960. Monumental problems had to be overcome. The biggest roadblocks, or at least the most heart-rending, were created by friends rather than enemies: suspicions, fears, slanders, betrayals, robberies, legalisms. I could go on. It would be a long and lugubrious list. The point is that one stout and sturdy passion turns that entire heap of unhappy obstacles into an inconsequential comedy of human foolishness. Such a comedy does not drive a man into depression; nor does it elicit a whimper or a snicker; it touches him at the pit of his being and evokes a belly laugh. And there is hardly anything more salubrious to the soul of man than uproarious belly laughter!

Passion for God has got to be fleshed out in concrete specific life projects. Mine—an unflinching determination since 1960—was to glorify God according to the authentic spirit of my Carmelite vocation and minister to the deepest and direst needs of my fellowman. I hope and pray that this concretely specified God-passion will never be snuffed out by the sins of my life but will burn on in my heart until my heart burns out for Him.

Purity of Heart

To be laid waste by one pure passion is to achieve simplicity and purity of heart. The Danish philosopher, Søren Kierkegaard, wrote a book called *Purity of Heart* and subtitled it, *To Will One Thing*. Nikos Kazantzakis wrote about a thirsty Moslem who came upon a well in the desert. He dropped a bucket into the well and pulled it up. It was full of silver. Emptying it, he dumped it into the well again and pulled it up full of gold. The Moslem protested: "My Lord God, I know how powerful you are and what marvels you are capable of! But all I want is a cup of water." He emptied the bucket of gold, lowered it into the well, and retrieved it. It was full of water. He drank and quenched his thirst. That is purity of heart!

Instead of the totally untenable concept of a "pure heart" that alledgedly never harbors any aggressive, sensuous or sexual thought, I suggest—as does the classic literature of mankind, including religious scriptures—that this term, rather, signifies the ability to feel life in all its depth, in joy as well as in sorrow. The "pure of heart" are those redoubtable champions of mankind who are willing to sense life in its total polarity. They are more like century plants or saguaro cactuses than drooping violets; more like roaring lions than bleating sheep. Such a broad-minded vision and wide range of feeling issuing in a profound experience of polarity is the true significance of the biblical search for "purity of heart" and the emotional foundation of all piety.

The stellar moments of human excellence were celebrated by mountain men who climbed to the pinnacle of passion, the mountaintop, and were there transfigured. These were men who matched their mountains. There are many such mountains. Some are famous: Horeb, Tabor, Calvary, Alverna, and Carmel.

The men who scaled these mountaintops and enjoyed such peak human experiences were, like the mountains themselves, ethereal and earthy, eerie and erotic. I mean erotic in the radical sense of that word, in its real meaning: a reaching and stretching with every fiber of one's body-person for the fullness of life. The phallic symbol seems to be an appropriate, though very partial, embodiment of this erotic thrust toward the utmost.

Climbing the mountain, not reaching the top, is the important thing. In fact, as Buddhists say, when you reach the top, keep climbing. Seeking is up to us. Finding is up to God. The ascent is our responsibility. The quality of our ascent depends upon the *mounting of our passion*. The climax depends upon God. St. John of the Cross' *Ascent of Mount Carmel* was originally a passionate poem and subsequently a masterful commentary on mounting passion.

The techno-barbaric juggernaut makes human participation in the fullness of life very difficult, makes the *Ascent of Mount Carmel* almost impossible. The dehumanized condition of man, his habitual torpor, and the debilitating pressures of his schizoid society are not conducive to mountain climbing, and militate against the human vocation: the persevering ascent toward the perfection of love. That is why I must add one more famous mountain, a mythical one, to my list of celebrated pinnacles of passion: Mount Sisyphus.

Man must not only deal with the external conditions and extrinsic pressures that impinge upon him. He must face up to his own internal possibilities. Albert Camus, French existentialist, was exceptionally good at this and enjoyed the gift of expressing it truthfully and shockingly. He was at home with fate. By fate I do not refer to misfortunes that befall us, but to the inevitable pain, anguish, and weakness of the human condition. The myth of Sisyphus presents man's fate in as stark a form as could be imagined. Just as Sisyphus reaches the top of the mountain, the rock he has arduously pushed ahead of him rolls to the bottom, and he must begin the struggle all over again. Camus finds in that fate, for the man who is brave and honest enough to accept the consciousness of it, something which evokes his passion for life, his will to be, his struggle for value and meaning, his undying effort to love:

> I leave Sisyphus at the foot of the mountain . . . . This universe without a master seems to him neither sterile nor futile. Each atom of that stone, each mineral flake of that night-filled mountain, in itself forms a world. The struggle itself toward the heights is enough to fill a man's heart. One must imagine Sisyphus happy. [3]

What is important is not vast achievement or triumphant victory, but endless effort. St. Teresa said: "Strive and strive and strive; we were meant for nothing else." That's right. There is such a thing as the triumph of failure—a failure of results. The triumph consists in persevering effort. God sanctifies us through our efforts, not our successes. Sisyphus represents the faithful commitment to nothing but God.

---

3. Albert Camus, *The Myth of Sisyphus* (New York: Alfred A. Knopf, 1955), p. 123.

The Final Love Affair: From Red Heat to White Heat

There is great passion in Shakespeare's *Romeo and Juliet*, Emily Brontë's *Wuthering Heights*, and Wagner's *Tristan und Isolde*. But somehow it is never quite enough. These romantic classics come close to describing the fire that Christ came to cast. But they don't quite make it. After all is said and done, after all the agony and ecstasy of romantic love, there is something dismal and dissatisfying about these great love stories. They are not mystical or luminous enough. Passion never really takes off. It is stymied and stunted by inevitable human limitations. It reminds me of faulty fire crackers and rockets that are ignited on the Fourth of July, that fill you with wondrous expectation as they hiss, crackle, and fume, but never explode, filling the sky with a riot of sparkle and color.

The passion of John of the Cross, on the other hand, broke through the barriers and transcended inherent perimeters. There was, indeed, an explosion and a take-off. You find in John, this towering mountain man of pure passion, a luminosity that outshines all the great love-lights of romantic literature. The power and life of his mystical poetry are a white heat of spiritual passion. That heat molds his imagery and burns through it. Every detail is ablaze with it, even "the breeze from the turret," "the lilies," and the "fanning cedars."

This passion of the mystic, the Christ-man, is significantly termed white heat in contradistinction to the red heat of a passion that is merely earthly and physical. The white heat of a man in love with God is far more intense than romantic red heat. The fire of the classical romantics, or of any great secular lover, may be more expansive and brilliant, but it pales before the concentrated intensity of St. John of the Cross's "living flame of love."

The singular coruscation of even romantic love is due to the erotic effort to transcend sensual love. It tends to pass over into the spiritual passion of an infinite love. Eros almost turns into agape. It cannot, however, free itself from subjection to its finite object, from bondage to its sensual conditions. And so the love affair, typified in the great episodes of romantic literature, as well as in the more fragile instances of contemporary art forms, however promising, ends in tragedy, a tragedy not really due to its external circumstances, but inherent in its very nature. The mystic leaps beyond the boundaries into the mystery. Or, if you will, having exhausted the powers of eros, he is lifted by the Inexhaustible Spirit into agape and in that divine realm he begins to envision and inhale the impossible possibilities or the possible impossibilities of love.

It takes a man of John of the Cross's stature, a superb poet and a supernal mystic, to unite so intimately the earthly type and the spiritual antitype, to fuse so completely the most vehement passion with perfect purity. The purity of John's blazing passion was obtained, and is only obtainable, by a total mortification and relentless crucifixion of the flesh and its desires. St. John scaled the summit of Mount Carmel not on his own steam, but on the power of the Spirit of God in him (agape), a Spirit rooted in and embodied by his own natural and unstinting quest for supreme value (eros).

As St. John points out, there is only one entrance into the mystical life. That entry is the Dark Night. In the Dark Night the passion flames forth unchecked by any barrier because it is perfectly pure—and purity is essentially freedom from limits. That is why mystics, men and women who plow through the tumultuous upheavals and torrential storms of the Dark Nights, are the most passionate of all people, exploring, as they do, the terrible uncharted regions of human evolution.

Passion is simply life in its most intense vigor. But people are afraid of passion because they are afraid of life. They blame passion for the limits they refuse to vault. Passion is the breakthrough virtue. If passion remains unspent, the limits remain unleveled. In this way, passionlessly, apathetically, we permit the natural boundaries of our life to enclose and enslave us. We allow finite structures themselves to distort and sully life in fallen sensebound humanity.

The Incarnation, the life of Christ, was the passion of God breaking through decisively. Human boundaries were pushed back ad infinitum. All things were made new. If I have a spiritual life, that means that I am immersed in the life of the wild and insuppressible Spirit transcending all the bastions of the empirical, separative, and lamentably limited ego.

We slink away from the challenge of the spiritual life. We take refuge in a cold and uninspired moralism and in an artificially closed circle of thought and practice. Consequently, the

stream of life leaves us behind in its backwaters as it sweeps on-
wards, a turbid, muddy, often destructive, but always swirling
force. The result: a mediocre world of nice people. How pitiful!
We lack the capacity to purify and spiritualize passion and therefore must avoid it entirely. So what help can we be to those who
will and must live with the fullness of life, and must love passionately? They are the ones who need to be fed, helped, and directed,
led irrevocably all the way up the mountain. But we would rather
dally and dither in the meager foothills pandering to the tiny
passions of inert masses of lukewarm people.

The saints are the bold ones, daring enough to be different,
humble enough to make mistakes, wild enough to be burnt in
the fire of love, real enough to make the rest of us see how enormously phony we are. They transform passion and raise it to a
higher level where it is freed from the strictures of sense. They
are passionate pilgrims of the Absolute, restless until they rest
in an infinite love that is the intense passion of pure Spirit. If
they seem to withdraw, it is only for the sake of a fuller life from
which the limits of that lower life would have debarred them.

The saints do not confine emotion and passion to the sense-
condition activities of the soul. This would eliminate philosophical
eros and theological agape. Such a tendency would substitute as
an ideal the apathy of the Stoic for the holy abandonment of the
Christian. It would turn vital, adventurous mystics into stuffed
shirts.

The spiritual passion of the Dark Night exceeds the passion
of earthly love as the fire of the sun, the fire of a candle. Life is
love passionate and intense. Only in such love is reality touched—
the rest is deception, bondage, and spiritual death. Such love
draws upwards, ever more persistently, to the mountain peaks.
The fulfilled passion of St. John passes into the peace of perfect
satisfaction, its energy spent in ecstatic absorption rather than in
sporadic desire. In this mystic marriage are fulfilled all knowledge
and all art, all striving, all desire, all love, and all life. This spousal
union is the limitless Being of God eternally filling the virginal
emptiness of the soul. It is harmony without striving, love without
longing, yes without no, and life without death.

The Elijan Spirit

It must be obvious by now that Mount Carmel is my favorite mountain and St. John of the Cross my favorite mountain man. He inspired me to become a Carmelite. Carmel seemed to present an eminent possibility for a full life in passionate pursuit of the All.

St. Matthew makes an extraordinary statement about John the Baptist, which is also applicable to John of the Cross:

> Ever since the coming of John the Baptist, the Kingdom of Heaven has been subjected to violence, and violent men are seizing it. For all the prophets and the Law foretold things to come until John appeared, and John is the destined Elijah, if you will but accept it (Mt. 11:12-13).

John of the Cross, too, is unmistakably Elijah. Elijah himself is "a figure of absolutely primeval force," according to renowned Scripture scholar, Gerhard von Rad. He is consumed with zeal for the Lord God of hosts. He will not compromise or tolerate rival gods. He is so self-full (not selfish) that he almost seems arrogant. His composure gives the impression of downright inertia. But it was an impassioned composure. God was always loving Israel and forever ready to prove it, and Elijah knew that. Israel did not need to seek God's attention or beg for it in fussy, raving ways. God was already hot in pursuit. Israel needed a man sufficiently wild and wise to face up to his jealous claims and cushion his relentless love blows. Man cannot bear much reality. Elijah accepted full responsibility for his unshakable independent selfhood. God was no prop for him, no alibi, no resting place. He was the Mighty, Mysterious One who induced him to come up with an unmitigated beingful stance. That's what Israel needed in order to cope with God: that's what we need. It is what I would call the *Elijan spirit*.

There was no hope for all Israel, only for a remnant—the passionate ones who were touched and lived by the Elijan spirit. Because of the remnant, the few who remained faithful, God was not finished with Israel. Yahweh would "spare seven thousand, all the knees that had not bowed to Baal, and every mouth that had not kissed him" (1 Kgs. 19:18). It was only through this passionate remnant that Israel endured at all. The same is true of the Church today, kept alive by a remnant. The few really live people in touch with God hold things together and keep the world from falling apart. It has always been thus:

> Noah and his sons are simply a remnant preserved: Lot and his family are the same, a remnant escaped from Sodom: Jacob divided his possessions in such a way that, if the worse came to the worst, the company which was left might be a "remnant which escaped" (Gen. 22:9): and in a solemn hour Joseph declared to his brethren that the reason why Yahweh had led him in that strange way he had was "in order to preserve a remnant on earth, and to keep you alive as a great remnant which escaped" (Gen. 45:7). The only new thing in Elijah's use of the concept is that he refers it to preservation from calamities which are still to come and which Yahweh himself is to bring about.[4]

Elijah is not a typical biblical "subject" or "figure." He is more like an august event: the eye of a storm, the place where lightning strikes, the ravages of a tornado. We remember Elijah the way we remember the Alamo or the Chicago Fire or the Irish Rebellion. He was the way God's passion broke through the pallid world of miserable man, and still does. Elijah was no pompous religious figure. He described himself as one who "attends upon Yahweh as servant" (1 Kgs. 18:15). God simply used his servant at a momentous hour. The time in which Elijah lived was rife with miracles, but he himself never worked one. A far greater achievement is to be available, expendable, wholly and always there. That is passion, and it is the white heat of the Elijan spirit caught and communicated to the whole world in the life, poetry and mysticism of St. John of the Cross.

---

4. Gerhard von Rad, *Old Testament Theology* (New York: Harper and Row, 1965), p. 22.

One of my favorite contemporary Elijans, Greek author Nikos Kazantzakis, sums it up magnificently:

> Blowing through heaven and earth, and in our hearts and the heart of every living thing, is a gigantic breath—a great Cry—which we call God. Plant life wished to continue its motionless sleep next to stagnant waters, but the Cry leaped up within it and violently shook its roots: "Away, let go of the earth, walk!" Had the tree been able to think and judge it would have cried, "I don't want to. What are you urging me to do? You are demanding the impossible!" But the Cry, without pity, kept shaking its roots and shouting, "Away, let go of the earth, walk!"
>
> It shouted in this way for thousands of eons; and lo! as a result of desire and struggle, life escaped the motionless tree and was liberated.
>
> Animals appeared—worms—making themselves at home in water and mud. "We're just fine," they said, "We have peace and security; we're not budging."
>
> But the terrible Cry hammered itself pitilessly into their loins. "Leave the mud, stand up, give birth to your betters!"
>
> "We don't want to! We can't!"
>
> "You can't, but I can. Stand up!"
>
> And lo! After thousands of eons, man emerged, trembling on his still unsolid legs.
>
> The human being is a centaur; his equine hoofs are planted in the ground, but his body from breast to head is worked on and tormented by the merciless Cry. He has been fighting, again for thousands of eons, to draw himself, like a sword, out of his animalistic scabbard. He is also fighting— this is his new struggle—to draw himself out of his human scabbard. Man calls in despair: "Where can I go? I have reached the pinnacle, beyond is the abyss." And the Cry answers, "I am beyond. Stand up!" All things are centaurs. If this were not the case, the world would rot into inertness and sterility.[5]

Nikos's Cry becomes strikingly meaningful once we have assimilated into our concept of the Whole Christ our recently ac-

---

5. Nikos Kazantzakis, *Report to Greco* (New York: Simon and Schuster, 1965), pp. 278-279.

quired knowledge of evolution and depth-psychology.

We are meant to pick up where Jesus left off and thus "to fill up what is wanting to the passion of Christ" (Col. 1:24), becoming in our own way for the twentieth century, for the humanization and deification of man, what Jesus was in the first. Like him, we are the "annointed" ones of God, so divinely loved, pleasured, energized that we can make all things brand new.

Passion issues in resurrection. Resurrection means freedom —now; the freedom to live by love. It is love that evokes life and gives it an eternal dimension. We must not stand before the empty tomb but attend to some poor derelict in whom the dead Christ awaits resurrection.

2: Divine Passion

Are there any more crucial words in the English language than "the love of God?" The phrase refers to both God's concern for us and our longing for him. Both references are supremely important, each one lavishly laden with the essential ingredients of life itself. But how hackneyed this superb summary of the human adventure has become! One is apt to hear more tripe and hogwash on "the love of God" than on any other subject. It is a pity that man slips so easily and stupidly into profanities and pietisms. Imagine the powerful effect if men and women resorted to either a profane or pious expression maybe twice in a lifetime! That would be a momentous occasion and a trenchant bit of communication.

God himself communicates with us only in trenchant terms. Precisely because of his passion, God speaks only one word, his whole Word, and it remains unutterable and unalterable, except in its singular Christic embodiment. Yahweh proclaims himself *El Kana*, a passionate God, panting with pure, holy lust after man whom he loves; and he demands *ahabah*, the very same word used in the Song of Songs to describe the sexually aroused love of the bride and groom.

The etymology of the word "Allah" indicates the same sort of thing: a strong, powerful feeling in God that is bountiful and substantial, not partial and sentimental. The sacred name derives the word *ilah* from the root w/h connoting to be sad, to be overwhelmed with sadness, to sigh toward, to flee fearfully toward. Even God seems to be deeply moved by his precarious closeness to man whom he loves, respects, and needs—however freely. The very meaning of his name yields a little of the secret of his being. God is a hidden treasure, so inscrutable, unfathomable. With an unslaked passion for revelation, active and passive, he yearns to know and to be known, creating creatures precisely to be loved by them. It is this divine passion that underlies the entire divine dramaturgy, the eternal cosmogony.

17

In its essence every existent is a breath of the existentiating divine passion, and so an individual embodiment of compassion. Every bit of genuine, unselfish feeling in the universe issues from the divine pathos of the Godhead; and it is sympathy (*sympathos*) that unites the adorable God with the adoring worshiper in compassionate dialogue; and all valid forms of ministry, enlightened service, spring from this vital source.

This pathos is far more than mercy toward a servant or indulgence and forgiveness shown the sinner. Every creature is created by it and refined by it, uplifted by it; and, ultimately, all will be fulfilled by it.

Since God graciously describes himself to me through myself I do not often beg him to be compassionate with me, but implore him to let his divine compassion inundate the world through me. I may be next to nothing, but since God is Pure Being and is at present passionately aspiring *to be* through and for me, I who am at prayer can become the very organ of his passion. "Make me a compassionate one, O Lord; become through me what from all eternity you have desired to be." My prayer is not so much a request as an actual mode of being in his presence. Growth in that kind of existential prayer is increased capacity for God.

In this context, reference to a person as "the image and likeness of God" is no longer a cliché because such a person, even though a sinner, has become a compassionate one, experiencing infinite sadness over undisclosed virtualities and embracing in an act of total religious sympathy the theophanies of God in all faiths and in all instances of human becoming.

The Bible is a love story, the story of God creating out of nothing but love. Out of this creative love he fashions himself a world, a people, a bride, a son, a church. From the original breath, "a mighty wind that swept over the surface of the waters" (Gn. 1:2), to the last crucified cry over Jerusalem, the passion of God broke through all worldly blockades and human impediments, until it raised up Jesus from the dead. Through Christ's victory over death all men are divinely empowered to free themselves from every human bondage and so to live in love with the All. That is the final breakthrough. And it takes forever.

Personal Passionate Presence

God so loved the Hebrews that he chose to make this one people his own, and this election is an historical intervention, an irruption of divine passion in the human domain, binding with zeal and jealousy a particular people to himself. Once the covenant is established, God's care for and faithfulness to his fickle and faltering people is his *hesed*, his loving kindness, his steadfast love, or his mercy. *Hesed* was a potent word among the Hebrews. It always referred to some kind of *pledged passion*, for instance, the fidelity of Ruth to Naomi, the blood-brotherhood between David and Jonathan or the covenant between God and man ratified by Abraham.

God's love affair with Israel is nothing if it is not passionate. The metaphors and expressions of human love between parent and child and between husband and wife are fundamental in the speech about the love of God. The underlying theme of all that the Old Testament has to say about the active, processive development of the God-man relation can be found in the obviously pervasive pattern of a *personally passionate presence*, characterized by intense devotion and loyalty. Sacred History is the turbulent and tumultuous record of love between God and his people.

Jeremiah, like the other prophets, regarded the time in the wilderness as a time of purity and loyalty in the life of Israel: "Thus says the Lord: I remember the devotion of your youth, your love as a bride, how you followed me in the wilderness, in the land not sown" (Jer. 2:2). God not only woos and entices Israel into a covenant of love, but overpowers Jeremiah himself: "O Lord, Thou hast seduced me, and I am seduced; Thou hast raped me, and I am overcome" (Jer. 20:7). The prophet was both frightened and fascinated by this experience of the numinous, by this overwhelming overture of infinite love. His response was one of solemn terror and sheer delight. "Thy words were found and I ate them, Thy words became to me a joy, the delight of my heart, for I am called by Thy name, O Lord, God of hosts" (Jer. 15:16). But we know the weakness and wickedness of man, recorded in the tragic infidelities and idolatries of Israel. Hosea uses the metaphor of harlotry to describe Israel's defection from Yahweh's love.

"In the house of Israel I have seen a horrible thing. Ephraim's harlotry is there, Israel is defiled" (Hos. 1:10).

In Hosea, in the magnificent eleventh chapter especially, we find in God's passion for Israel both sides of love: tender compassion and wrathful indignation. Judgment and punishment are an integral part of divine love in the Old Testament. God's wrath and punishment are always reasonable and fitting and are therefore appropriate expressions of divine pathos. The biblical language does seem vindictive and exaggerated, it is true, but it is the exaggeration of a righteous indignation. What calls forth God's wrath is the violation of the covenant of love that he has established. This is the fundamental connection between love and judgment.

What Yahweh demands from the person and the people he loves is not some part or parcel of the human being, or of the human race, to be sealed off and sacrificed to the absolute requirements of the deity as a recognition and mitigation of his severe exactions; what he wants is what total love always wants, however freely and patiently: the whole man and his whole world all of the time, with no division, no compromise, no holding back. The prophetic pronouncements make this clear.

God's passion for Israel is the exemplar of his love relationship with all of mankind. This is not sufficiently explicit in the Hebrew Scripture due to the limitations of the revealing instruments, the inspired writers of the Bible. But God created *all* men in his divine image. Universalistic passages which suggest that God's concern for all nations is of the same character as for Israel do occur, for example, in Amos 9:7, Zechariah 8:23, Jonah, Ruth, Isaiah 19:19-25, 42:1-6, and 47:6. The same theme is also neatly reflected in a Talmudic story. When the Egyptians are drowning in the Red Sea and the angels want to sing, God rebukes them: "My handiwork is dying, and you wish to sing?"[1] A far cry from the Israelites' revelry with tambourines and dancing described in Exodus 15!

This obscure passion-of-God theme becomes clear in Christ who "divides the men from the boys," that is, the mystics from the romantics. Jesus leads the Jews to the brink. What is required

---

1. Lewis I. Newman, ed. *Talmudic Anthology* (New York: Behrman House, 1945), p. 144.

of them at this crucial juncture is a daredevil leap into the abyss of his mystery, an unquestionable affirmation of the unbounded universality of his love. The only alternative is a disastrous denial. We are poignantly aware of just how disastrous this denial is by noting the multiple forms of regressive tribalism to which an undaring, distrusting humanity has succumbed. This is a crisis situation that every developing person or nation must face. Waterloos and Watergates abound here. But if we take the leap beyond private preoccupations—personal or national—we *passover* from romanticism to mysticism. The final breakthrough embraces everyone. Passion for the unity of all is the ultimate passion. If revelation is the passion of God breaking through, then Christ is the definitive breakthrough.

The Lion Story

The final breakthrough is described as the victory of a mighty lion in the traditions of both East and West. "As for the lion which you saw coming from the forest, roused from sleep and roaring . . . this is the Messiah whom the Most High has kept back until the end," claimed the priest-scribe Esdras in an apocryphal writing only a few hundred years before the birth of Christ. "He will be merciful to those of my people that remain . . .; he will set them free and give them gladness" (2 Esdras 12:31-34). In more recent times, Swami Vivekananda speaks in the same terms:

A lioness in search of prey came upon a flock of sheep, and as she jumped at one of them, she gave birth to a cub and died on the spot. The young lion was brought up like a sheep, and it never knew that it was a lion. One day a lion came across the flock and was astonished to see in it a huge lion eating grass and bleating like a sheep. At his sight the flock fled and the lion-sheep with them. But the lion watched his opportunity and one day he found the lion-sheep asleep. He woke him up and said, "You are a lion." The other said, "No," and began to bleat like a sheep. But the stranger lion took him to a lake and asked him to look in the water at his own image and see if it did not resemble him, the stranger lion. He looked and

acknowledged that it did. Then the stranger lion began to roar
and asked him to do the same. The lion-sheep tried his voice
and soon was roaring as grandly as the other. And he was a
sheep no longer.[2]

The Lion Story is another version of the Bible story. It's the
story of the Exodus, the Passover, the deliverance of the people of
God from the enslavement of Egypt. It took a wild, "wanted,"
passionate man, seized by the fury of God, to free the Israelites
from the Egyptian slavery to which they had grown accustomed.
Once liberated they fell into other forms of disgraceful bondage so
that other prophets of the same indomitable spirit of Moses had to
rise up and reform the people of God, lest they lose their image
and likeness of the deity and become, by the force of sheer habit,
immutable slaves once again.

Out of this resolute race came one who was more than a
prophet. He was a special kind of man. Jesus became the Christ,
the free man, the God-man, and therefore, the liberator, the di-
vinizer, the pontiff: the bridge to freedom and the way to deification. The Lion Story is above all the story of Christ who recognized that he was no sheep and could roar like a lion! When he
perceived the divinity within him, our pristine unfettered humanness was restored; in fact, it was infinitely improved. Christ
came "that we might have life and have it more abundantly"
(John 10:10). He instituted what we call the Church (a pack
of lions) to keep this wild, exuberant, and divine vitality alive in
the world forever.

After the Ascension, however, the baby lions Christ left behind were overwhelmed by the huge number of sheep compared
with the paucity of lions. Impressed by the fact that sheep are
protected in safe, lush places and fed regularly, even though eventually led to slaughter, they crept back into the sheepfolds. By the
fourth century there were only a few wild, roaring lions left, and
with some exceptions they survived only in the wilderness. You
could hardly tell the difference between the average, nice, tame
lion and the sheep of the flock with which he merged.

At the great Sheep Center, Constantinople, in the year 325,

2. Swami Vivekananda, *The Complete Works of Swami Vivekananda,*
Vol. 1 (Mayavati: Advaita Ashrama, 1955), pp. 324-325.

a terrible thing happened. The leader of the lions felt it was better
to live sheepishly in the plush pastures of the sheep and bleat like
a lamb than to live the daring, dangerous life of a majestic beast
roaring and rampaging in the wilderness. So he made a deal with
the head of the sheep. Ever since, all "decent" lions graze and
bleat like sheep. Their leaders keep meeting and rearranging
leonine life-styles, updating and modernizing, striving for respectable forms of activity and meaningful relationships among themselves and with the sheep, trying with all their diminished might
to preserve some semblance of lionhood while enjoying all the ad-
vantages of the sheepfold.

Every once in a while a wild lion saunters into the fold. Both
the tame lions and the sheep notice what a colossal beast he is,
mighty and magnificent from eating strong meat in the wilderness
and exercising all of his lion potential; they all shiver and shake
when he roars.

The mini-lions feel terribly embarrassed and frightfully in-
secure. So they manage either to expel him or devise a way to
have him killed—as legally as possible.

Lions have behaved like lambs for so long now that it seems
right and proper for them to eat grass and bleat like sheep. In
fact, a whole fancy, complicated network called "law and order"
has been set up in and around the sheepfold to protect and preserve the status quo of the mini-lions. It is called the code of Lion
Law. But the crucial influence and critical criteria for both lion
and sheep codes come from the same source: the middle-class
herd. The whole sheepish rigmarole of rule and ritual that en-
ables mini-lions to live in numerical abundance has made it almost impossible for the few real lions to survive.

The life of the Church in the world today resembles the life
of mini-lions in a sheepfold. We sheepishly stunt our growth and
stifle our lives in a convulsive effort to fit the infinite foolishness of
God and the marvelously mad, lusciously lovely enfleshment of
divine folly—the body of Christ—into this cribbed and cramped
politico-religious world of ours.

The Church has so compromised her position that many of
her activities seem to be nothing more than the writhings of an
impaled creature. We all stand around looking at the victim
dumbfoundedly, writing about it, discussing it, or organizing it.

The opinion of so many mesmerized observers, glib writers, the timeless talkers, and the frantic organizers seems to be that if the Church squeaks and squirms enough she will find her place in the world again and be granted a certain dignity and prestige. I hope they are wrong. Nothing nullifies the mission of the Church so effectively as the condescending approval of the world.

Jesus became what it was in him from the beginning to become, the Christ, the Lion of Judah, the God-man. He broke out of the sheepfold and roams round the world; his mission is to liberate and deify all those bold and willing enough to follow him.

As natural and as human as we are, one of our own has made it. He is God. And he made it perfectly clear by the way he spoke and lived that all of us are meant to be transformed and deified. "Ye are gods," he said (John 10:34); and "You will do greater things than I" (John 14:12).

He is both the magnetic force pulling us toward our ultimate destiny and the infinitely terrifying and delightful model of the existential way it happens. What exactly was it that moved him from the fabulously fertile lowlands where the mini-lions grazed languidly with the sheep to the austere and awesome mountaintops where even the wildest and bravest lions would not go? What empowered him to leap beyond all human boundaries and plunge into the divine abyss? What enabled him to free us from everything except love once we follow him all the way?

There is one simple answer: his passion. Not a plurality of passions—that's what dissipates, fragments, and immobilizes the rest of us; but a singular passion that swept over him like a tidal wave, quickened every fiber of his body, stirred his soul to the depths, brought together, and, to a boil, all his emotional energy, and marshalled all the forces of his erotic being into an intellectual act of unconditional and universal love of God. Nothing of him or the scabrously raw matter of his being-in-the-world was left out of that undivided love. He was touched—consumed—at the very core of his personality by the Triune love, which is not only the most solemn, serious and sacred love in the world, but the most sexual, since the persons of the Trinity live and thrive eternally and are constituted in being by their altruistic relatedness. Directed by no other force than Love, one passionate purpose initiated, motivated, and culminated the life of Christ: his Father's will.

By Christ's passion I mean much more than the final Way of the Cross ending in his murder on Golgotha. I mean more than three days of passion. By Christ's passion I mean his positive and purposeful readiness to suffer the whole of life: the onslaughts of divine love *(pati divina)* and the exigencies of human becoming *(pati humana)*. There was nothing negative or pitiful about Christ's suffering. He did not, like a pathetic victim, let too many things happen to him. He did not allow the circumstances and conditions of the day to rule his life but took matters into his own hands and was responsible for the direction of his own life. He was not a lamb but a lion.

The Suffering God

The Lord's passion embodies and makes so visible and tangible nothing other than the *suffering of God*. An analytical and purely rational cast of mind tends to reduce the living God of Abraham, Isaac, and Jacob to abstract and lifeless concepts. This unfortunate tendency goes way back to St. Augustine who comes close to glorifying a certain complacency in the divine love, or what Anders Nygren's study, *Agape and Eros*, goes so far as to call egocentricity. This unhappy concept of the nature of God grew out of an important and necessary determination on the part of Augustine and the other Church Fathers to preserve the absolute fullness and independence of God's being. This they achieved by combining the God of the Bible with the absolute of neoplatonic metaphysics. The unfortunate but inevitable effect of this wedding was the serious diminution and sometimes disappearance of the active, temporal, creating, suffering side of God's being.

For Augustine, as well as for the subsequent Thomistic tradition, all things are caught up in the predetermined web of God's absolute, nontemporal, impassible, unchanging power. But with a renewed biblical perspective in conjunction with our recent evolutionary and depth-psychological perspectives, we should have no trouble reconceiving the meaning of God's being in relation to time and history. In fact, I would dare say that until the suffering God concept is understood and assimilated, not many people are going to enjoy passionate love affairs with God or live worldly lives of prayer. And if love affairs with God are not passionate and prayer-lives are not worldly, they are not worth our while.

God who is love is certainly not static but infinitely dynamic; not remote, but more me than I am. It is the nature of love to be moved by the conditions of the beloved. God, then, must be the most *moved* Mover as well as being the *unmoved* Mover. This is a complex philosophical problem, I know, but since a full-fledged prayer-life in and for the world as well as enlightened and passionate love of God depend on our true grasp of this reality, we cannot afford to be skittish.

God is, as Christian theology has always insisted, impassible. Impassible simply means that God cannot be acted upon against his will. He is perfectly flexible but does not fluctuate; he is magnificently supple but cannot be supplemented.[3]

The prophets proclaim that God is deeply moved with compassion at human need or with indignation at man's greed. It is God who "feels fiercely" and the prophet is in sympathy with him. The Jewish scholar and famed Rabbi, Abraham Heschel, afraid of a sentimental interpretation of God's "feelings," employs a technical term, "the divine pathos." Heschel claims that God's unconditional concern for justice is not an anthropomorphism. Man's concern for justice is a theomorphism. He is in agreement with Dietrich Bonhoeffer's affirmation: "Only the suffering God can help."

A scene toward the end of Miss Helen Waddell's *Peter Abelard* portrays with particular poignancy this idea of the suffering God. Peter and Thibault are in the woods and hear a terrible cry like the scream of a child in agony. Finding a rabbit caught in a trap, they free it; it nuzzles into Peter's arms, and dies.

> It was the last confiding thrust that broke Abelard's heart . . . "Thibault," he said, "do you think there is a God at all? Whatever has come to me, I earned it. But what did this one do?" Thibault nodded. "I know," he said. "Only—I think God is in it too." Abelard looked up sharply, "In it?

---

3. Disciples of Whitehead and Process Philosophers have developed this basic insight into the processive nature of God. The theologian most helpful to me on this difficult subject has been the late Daniel Day Williams, Professor of Theology at Union Theological Seminary in New York. I am particularly indebted to *The Spirit and Forms of Love* (New York: Harper and Row, 1968).

Do you mean that it makes him suffer the way it does us?"
Again Thibault nodded . . . "All this," he stroked the limp
body, "is because of us. But all the time God suffers. More
than we do." Abelard looked at him, perplexed. "Thibault, do
you mean Calvary?" Thibault shook his head. "That was
only a piece of it—the piece that we saw—in time. Like that."
He pointed to a fallen tree beside them, sawn through the middle. "The dark ring there, it goes up and down the whole
length of the tree. But you only see where it is cut across. That
is what Christ's life was; the bit of God that we saw. And we
think God is like that forever, because it happened once with
Christ. But not the pain. Not the agony at the last. We think
that stopped." Abelard looked at him . . . "Then, Thibault,"
he said slowly, "you think that all this . . . all the pain of the
world, was Christ's cross?" "God's cross," said Thibault.
"And it goes on." "The Patripassion heresy," muttered Abelard mechanically. "But, oh God, if it were true, Thibault, if it
were true. Thibault, it must be. At least, there is something at
the back of it that is true. And if we could find it—it would
bring back the whole world."[4]

"Christ," says Paschal, "is in agony until the end of the
world; we must not rest in the meantime." In other words, Jesus,
who is both God and man, is the way between them. His agony
and his anxiety pave the way. He makes one thing absolutely
clear: man reaches God the same way God reaches man—by suffering. There is no alternative. Every other direction is a way out:
a clever device, a subtle dodge, a detour from the Way of the
Cross. That is why St. Francis told Brother Leo: "There is no
way—leap." To leap lustily into life is to follow Christ. This is
how one extends the boundaries of the mind beyond the reaches of
reason and unites the head and the heart, the sacred and the secular, the natural and the supernatural, in a pure intuition of God
born of love. Such a reconciliation of opposites issues in the transfiguration of man and the world. The anguished cry of Habakkuk
is often our own:

> How long, Yahweh, am I to cry for help
> while you will not listen;

---

4. Helen Waddell, *Peter Abelard: A Novel* (New York: Viking Press,
1959), pp. 263-265.

to cry "Oppression!" in your ear
and you will not save?
Why do you set injustice before me,
why do you look on where there is tyranny?
Outrage and violence, that is all I see,
all is contention, and discord flourishes.
And so the law loses its hold,
and justice never shows itself.
Yes, the wicked man gets the better of the upright,
and so justice is seen to be distorted.

(Habakkuk 1:1-4)

Jerusalem is destroyed by pagan powers and God does nothing. The ovens of Buchenwald are hot with human flesh and God does nothing. The jungles of the East are red with blood and God does nothing. The peoples of South America are annihilated by flood and hurricane and God does nothing. Hundreds starve to death daily in Bangladesh and God does nothing. The mighty and the unremembered fall, the widow weeps, the children stand mute with misunderstanding, and God does nothing.

Dietrich Bonhoeffer helps us understand what it is that God is "doing":

> God is teaching us that we must live as men who can get along very well without him. The God who is with us is the God who forsakes us (Mark 13:34). . . . God allows himself to be edged out of the world and onto the cross. God is weak and powerless in the world, and that is exactly the way, the only way, in which he can be with us. . . . Man's religiosity makes him look in his distress to the power of God in the world . . . the Bible however, directs him to the powerlessness and suffering of God: only a suffering God can help.[5]

Most authors who have in the recent past referred to Bonhoeffer's famous statement have quoted the eminent German scholar unfairly, and, in part, in support of their own already outmoded "death of God" theology. The quote *in toto* establishes un-

---

5. Dietrich Bonhoeffer, *Letters and Papers from Prison*, ed. by E. Bethge, tr. by R. Fuller. (New York: The Macmillan Co., 1962), p. 218.

equivocally the centrality of God's vital presence in the world. But God is so purely actual, he needs no feathering, no buttressing. He is so self-effacing in his creative act that only passionate, intuitive lovers notice.

If God is, he is responsible; if not as actual perpetrator, then as "eternal bystander," to use Peter Berger's phrase. Sometimes he seems to do nothing precisely because of the totality of his presence, the pure naked fact of his being there. As Lao Tzu says, the most important thing to do is nothing. The most important thing to do is to be. Being there is what God does. He is there burning in the ovens, bleeding in the jungles, drowning in the swollen rivers, dying of starvation, amidst the fallen, the weeping widows, the dumbfounded children. The closest God comes to defining himself is in the terms of *being there.* He does not say, "I am that I am" but as Martin Buber translates it, "I shall be there as I shall be there." P. Thornborough pleads for this kind of presence in a recent poem:

O God, O Nameless Something
That which contains all things,
Yet is not contained
Be there . . .
What is this that feels there should be meaning?
Something through and beyond the pain and cruelty
Ravaging this world?
Is it You? . . .
And is it You in the darkness of our minds
the injustice, the cruelty, the hurricane?
Can it be You in the Evil?
Are You buried there?
You who permeate the universe and beyond
Gloriously transcendental and yet immediately immanent
Within the minutest particle?
O God, O Nameless Something
Be there.

For apart from You, the ground of being
And the Transcendental mystery
There is no meaning;
And cruelty and evil remain,
And pain itself is meaningless.

O God, O Nameless Something
Help me to trust
Not blindly, still walking in uncertainty
But in trust for the journey
In, through, and out of the desert.

O God, O Nameless Something
Be there. [6]

The "suffering servant" God experienced by Isaiah and the prophets, revealed by Christ, and imaged in the soul is no self-sufficient autocratic potentate ruling the world from above, totally independent of man's own striving and seeking, indifferent to the profound passion of his eros. God suffers in the broken-hearted mother, the child crippled with birth defects, the sick old alcoholic, the prisoner, the beggar, the lonely spinster and the tormented soul. God suffers in history. The whole cosmos "groans and travails in pain" until all things are "summed up in Christ."

That is all we need to know: that in the passionate presence of the loving God "we live and move and have our being." Christ is both the verification and mediation of that presence. Only in Christ can I stand still and be myself in the reeling, bellowing world. He alone has the words of eternal life. Why drown in minor concerns and smaller joys? The oyster is here, the oyster with the Great Pearl (Mt. 13:45-46).

Christ is not the harbor where one casts anchor, but the harbor from which one departs, gains the offing, encounters a wild, tempestuous sea, and then struggles for a lifetime to anchor in God. Somewhere Nikos Kazantzakis goes on like this about the divine head of the Church. Christ is not the end but the beginning. He is not the "welcome" but the "bon voyage." He does not sit back restfully in soft clouds, but is battered by the waves just as we are, his eyes fixed aloft on the North Star, his hands firmly on the helm. Nikos claims that is why he likes him and why he would follow him. Me too.

If we follow closely enough in the footsteps of Christ we will catch his good infection and burn with the incandescent fire of his love. "I have come to bring fire to the earth, and how I wish it

6. P. Thornborough, "A Prayer," *New Christian*, April 2, 1970, p. 6.

were blazing already!'' (Luke 12:49). The Christ-infected man is purged of all his inhuman qualities, his vices, the way a moth gets rid of piggy-back vermin: he remains close enough to the white heat of a lamp for those ugly foreign particles to be burned away without being consumed himself. That's what happens when a man takes up his piggy-back cross and follows Christ. He is led into the presence of God where his impure accretions and all his egotisms are consumed in that Living Flame. Left with his naked self alone, nothing remains to isolate, separate, divide, or bog him down. He is in tune with God and all creatures: atonement. This amounts to a radical conversion that baptism merely initiates and adumbrates: an awakening in man of new springs of activity, a change in man's central direction and disposition.

The infection begins by recognizing the meaning of life as captured and conveyed in the Bible story, the basis and epitome of all love stories: God saying to me in action and in person over and over again, "I love you. I am with you. Fear not." That's not only the meaning of life but the creative cause of it—not once upon a time, but now.

"God, who in former times spoke in various ways to the fathers through the law and the prophets" (Heb. 1:1-2), spoke finally in the son. In that son, people recognized things about God, their world, their society, and themselves that they had not seen in that depth before. They concluded that in this son, Jesus, God was doing what they, as pious Jews, had been awaiting. And so, beginning there, "in Jerusalem and Judea," they were able to recognize God everywhere, "unto the uttermost parts of the earth" (Acts 1:8).

So it is today. If—as eclectic dilletantes do—I first seek God everywhere, in nature or in myself, I find very indistinct and sometimes contradictory clues. Nature seems to be as much bedeviled as Goddened. And an isolated search into myself is as liable to lead me into solipsistic introspection as it is to contemplation. I become captivated, not by the tremendous, fascinating mystery of God's self-disclosure, but by the intricacies of my own psyche and the reflection of my own face. But if I first find God in the historical Jesus, then I can rediscover nature numinously, catching the elusive inner reality of things. Nature then becomes crammd with God and his presence fills me. Then, too, without falling into the trap of psychidolatry, which tends to protect and sophisticate all forms of narcissistic introversion, I come to know by experience the true meaning of the scriptural statement: "The Kingdom of God is within you" (Luke 17:21).

Is the difference—the quality—we find in Jesus one of degree or of kind? The 19th-century Philosophers of Process help answer that. They noted that if one began adding to many realities in degree, they broke over at some unpredictable, critical point and became different in kind. Jesus exhibits more love and truth. But they are also unalloyed; which makes him a different kind of man, not just a better one.

Jesus is not the only revelation of God. But he is the indispensable and decisive one. He is the passion of God.

3: Christian Compassion

The passion of God meets and evokes the passion of man and through this com-passion of Christ-men, wherever they exist, the hard crust of the world is broken open and the Kingdom of God grows: love asserts itself at "the still point of the turning world."[1]

The word passion has an interesting history and takes on a very distinctive and highly significant meaning early in the Christian tradition. Originally, and particularly in Aristotelian usage, passion meant an affliction or seizure; it always implied suffering or passivity; ethically it was neutral: no one was praised or blamed for his passion. With the Stoics the passions came to be identified with restlessness. There was something tempestuous and disruptive about the passions. This meaning, more than the original, still influences our use of the word today, and has found its way into every moral system since the Stoics. Sometimes both the Aristotelian and Stoic meanings are combined, as in late Scholasticism, the philosophies of the Renaissance, and in the Church Fathers, in Augustine and Ambrose, for instance, whose Christian ethics were closer to the Stoic than the Aristotelian conception.

But from the very beginning, Christian authors introduced a fundamentally different meaning to the idea of passion. The Stoic, like the Buddhist, fled from the world in order to avoid suffering and passion. The Aristotelian opposed evil passions with good passions, striving by means of this rational compromise for a balanced position amidst the tumult of the world. The Christian came up with a brand new way of coping with the evil in the world, and that is by suffering: the glorious passion that springs from ardent love of God. To be passionate now meant to be immersed and engaged in life; to suffer life, not fecklessly but forcefully, and to transfigure matter with spirit: that is the function

---

1. T. S. Eliot, *Four Quartets* (New York: Harcourt, Brace and World, Inc., 1943), p. 15.

of passion. This willingness to suffer and die is a creative, dynamic force; in fact, it is the only source of rebirth, the single hope of
renewal in the world; and this notion of passion is of Christian
origin. The supreme instance of this royal and redemptive suffering is, of course, the passion of Christ. The cloud of witnesses
follow: the apostles, the martyrs, the solitaries, the celibates, and
all the saints driven by a reckless love to be identified with Christ
the high priest and victim.

    This distinctively Christian concept of passion, which we
find already highly developed in the inflamed life and letters of St.
Paul, reached a classical stage of development in St. Bernard and
in much of the subsequent Cistercian spirituality. It gave meaning
and value to the whole Franciscan way of life, finding dramatic
existential expression in the stigmata of St. Francis and eloquent
theological conceptualization in St. Bonaventure. About the same
time, St. Elizabeth of Hungary was plundering her palace to feed
the poor, preparing her body to pleasure her husband, and beg-
ging God to squander her. Not long afterwards Joan of Arc
showed the weary world and the crusty old Church what wild
passion it takes to become a saint. She managed it magnificently,
in accord with her own inner truth, by riding horses, leading soldiers to war, fighting battles, crowning kings, and being burnt at
the stake. Such sanctifying passion reached its flaming peak in the
undaunted conquistadores of the spiritual life, St. John of the
Cross and St. Teresa of Avila. And it flashed again in our own
century in the more pedestrian and imitable coruscation of St.
Therese's Little Way.

    The colossal saints are always the individuals whose passion
flames them to greatness. To paraphrase Thomas Carlyle, these
great men and women are always as lightning out of heaven; the
rest of men wait for them like fuel, and then they too will flame.
Three seem most appropriately representative of Carlyle's description: a celibate and disciple of Christ, Paul of Tarsus; a
married woman and mother, Elizabeth of Hungary; and a world-
shaking teenager and heroic feminist, Joan of Arc. It may be helpful to describe in some detail these models of Christian passion.

Love Letters of Wrath

Paul was a revolutionary on fire with the love of God, fascinated by Jesus and imbued with his Spirit. He could not tolerate man's ludicrous attempt to tame God and falsify love. God's presence is unbearable, his love immeasurable. It is something ever burning, breaking, making new.

When I was a theological student, we spent most of our time studying the Pauline Privilege, which is a tricky way out of a problematic marriage situation. We learned nothing of Pauline Passion. And all we ever heard about the passion of Christ was how it spent itself at the end in that long, lonely, agonizing walk up Mount Calvary.

An appreciation of Paul's passion would have rescued me long ago from measly pursuits. I've wasted so much time, for instance, writing inane, innocuous letters. From now on, I'm writing love letters. That doesn't mean mushy, sentimental stuff; it doesn't even mean pleasant. It means that I will address myself carefully and passionately to whomever I write about matters that deserve my loving attention. Nice people in a neatly run society often find such letters shocking, insulting, rude, righteous, vindictive, embarrassing, probably immoral, certainly improper. It isn't even safe to talk that way, they say; so why put it in writing? It's a risk, I know, but perhaps a prudent one since prudence means taking the best, not the safest, means to the proper end. Sometimes the best means are the unsafest.

Religious people are particularly finicky about what they write because they are supposed to be paragons of virtue which they equate with impeccable propriety. Such a dour outlook may force them to be morally upright, but certainly not great lovers.

I find the epistles of St. Paul so refreshing! They are love letters, vehement, volatile, but never irreverent. Paul is a thoroughly passionate man. And so are his letters passionate. He is passionate about God and the things that pertain to God, especially Christ and the members of his mystical body, the Church.

The passion of God has irrupted in the soul of Paul. The

divine pathos has laid hold of him. He is a marked man. Paul has seen God suffer. He made him suffer: "Saul, Saul, why do you persecute me?" (Acts 9:4). So love of God, according to Paul, is not all sweetness and light. His God is a God of love, but also a God of wrath. He warns us: "Observe the kindness and severity of God—severity to those who fall away, divine kindness to you, if only you remain within its scope" (Rom 11:22-23). And it is only against this background of wrath and severity that Paul speaks of love and goodness; otherwise his doctrine of divine agape would make no sense.

He who represents God, he who proclaims his word, is loving and wrathful at the same time. After all, he is passionately concerned and in anxiety that Christ be formed in those to whom he writes. This passion permeates his letters. One astonishing example is the marvelous mixture of valediction and malediction at the end of 1 Corinthians: "If anyone has no love for the Lord let him be anathema. Maranatha (may the Lord come)! The grace of the Lord Jesus be with you. My love be with you all in Christ Jesus" (1 Cor. 16:22-24).

Precisely because he is such a great lover there are things that Paul hates. And so we find him raging with anger against the Galatians. Nothing like the petty barbs of rancor and annoyance that sputter between a president and the members of the press and are televised across the nation, and nothing like the jejune pap that drips from some parish pulpits every Sunday or the pompous ecclesiastical pronouncements that make it so difficult for the Church to speak, in imitation of Christ, "with authority"! No, nothing like that, but strong invectives, denunciations and pleadings: "O fools of Galatians, who has bewitched you? . . . My little children, of whom I am in labor again" (Gal. 3:1; 4:19). This Pauline bombast mounts in fustigating fury until it reaches in the fifth chapter a paroxysm of vituperation: "I wish those who unsettle you would castrate themselves" (Gal. 5:12). A gentle suggestion, after all, since he leaves the decision up to them, unlike the suggestion of Billy Graham that convicted rapists be castrated by the state.

In Paul's letters there is a fundamental complementarity of love and hate. Each feeds the other and is intensified by the other. This fact is extremely significant. We foolishly tend to think of

God's love (agape) as nebulous and other-worldly. The truth is
that biblical agape is far more earthly, human, and worldly than
the Greek idealized eros. You will find a good explanation of this
in Kittel's New Testament *Theologisches Wörterbuch*:

> The essential characteristic of love in Israel is actually its
> tendency toward exclusiveness. The Greek eros is fundamen-
> tally universal, undiscriminating, undisciplined, broad-minded.
> The love which is commended in the Old Testament is a jeal-
> ous love which chooses one object among thousands and holds
> it fast with all the strength of its passion and its will, brooking
> no relaxation of the bond of loyalty. It is just this jealousy
> which reveals the divine strength of such love. It is no accident
> by which, in the Song of Songs (8:6) love strong as death is in-
> separably connected, in the poetic parallelism, with jealousy
> hard as hell. Jacob has two wives, but his love is given to only
> one of them (Gen. 29); he has twelve sons, but loves one of
> them more than all the others (Gen. 37:3). God has set many
> peoples in the world, but gives his love to the elect nation.
> With this he makes a covenant which he loyally keeps and
> jealously guards—as if it were a love of marriage (Hos. 1ff.).
> To break the law is a break of faith, to worship strange gods is
> adultery, calling forth the passionate jealousy of Yahweh . . .[2]

This selective and concrete channelling of love into a passionate and definite relationship with jealously guarded boundaries was not abrogated when Paul was knocked off his high horse
on the way to Damascus, turned totally and irrevocably to Christ
and joined his small community of believers. This Christ whom
he loved did not embody the god of universal amiability but the
God of Israel, with all his suprapersonal and possessive characteristics.

In fact, once Paul embraced the Christian faith that whole
central theme of the Bible, *passionate presence*, dominated his
personality and intensified his love-life in every possible way.
Having grasped significantly the ineluctable centrality of Em-
manuel, God with us, he understood with similar clarity the egre-

---

2. *Manuals from Kittel* Vol. 1: Love, trans. by Adam and Charles Black
(New York: Quell, Cottfried & Stauffer, 1949), pp. 32-33.

gious absurdity and arrogant imbecility of seeming to live without him. Sin, the rejection of God's love, the denial of his presence, came to be regarded by Paul as the most insane and inhuman act a man could possibly commit.

Every sin we inhumanly commit widens the gulf between "modern man" and the real world, the Kingdom of God established by Jesus Christ. What does this hideous gulf represent? It represents being at loggerheads with God: a disharmony with oneself, with others, with our natural environment, and with the One who suffuses it all and sustains it by his creative presence. Such conflict is the universal experience of mankind and remains unrectified until each one of us is remade, reborn, transfigured, Christened—call it what you will. This alone is dynamic revolution, the only effectively enduring and positively beneficial reformation in the history of the world.

That is why a renowned psychiatrist, Carl Menninger, wrote a book entitled *Whatever Happened to Sin?* It isn't the peccadillos Dr. Menninger is worried about. No one can completely avoid making mistakes and sometimes getting carried away. What is seriously damaging is the overall misdirection and disorientation of a lifetime. In this sense our omissions are very often worse than our commissions. So is our dalliance and our diffidence, and the accumulation of human diminishments.

Think of sin as the parallel of old people saying to the young, "You'll get over it, you won't mind it when you're my age." Think of sin as the drabness of life, the deadening of the spirit by routine, the killing of the spirit by the letter, the failure to live, to love, to adventure, as a kind of oldness, deadness, numbness, a fear of stepping out of line. Yet all this comes dramatically to an end on the cross. See death, and all is old and sad; see God in death, and all is suddenly new.

St. Paul said that the Law made sin worse. For when man sinned, the Law said, "Now you have had it. Now you have God against you," and this shut a man up inside his own sinfulness. But you don't worry about the Law when you have the wrath of God to contend with; and you know the gentle fury of God's wrath if you've had any experience of his love.

Man, without faith and hope in God's love, tends to hate God; and God hates what man has made of man. But God loves

Christ, and Christ loves God; Christ in God loves us, and we in Christ love God. This love is manifestly present in us if our relationships are animated by Christ's spirit, by the reverent, in-depth way we attend to one another.

God's persistent love, which is experienced as love by those who accept it in faith and hope, must be experienced as wrath by those who reject or ignore it. That is the teaching of St. John of the Cross who says that it is the same "Living Flame of Love" which purges, wounds and cauterizes, that also warms, soothes, and comforts. So Paul urges us to immerse ourselves in that divine love which casts out fear, but warns us of the divine wrath which summons us to accept that love. And the wrath of God is the inevitable consequence of God's passionate pursuit of man—this man, this nation—foolishly foiled by insouciance or insubordination. Reciprocally, the ardor, fervent constancy, and stunning fidelity of God's love is confirmed in Christ and revealed as unspeakably, immeasurably wonderful. The awful mystery of God disclosed in Christ is all the more ineffable. What a pathetic plight man would founder in forever without Christ! So Paul cannot afford to be pedantic, academic, disinterested. He is embroiled! And he is responsible. By the grace of God, divine pathos, he will overcome. And indeed, he does, attested to by the extraordinary evangelizing consequences of his prodigious energy.

So much of the love-talk today, including a good bit of the verbosity and tactility elicited in sensitivity sessions and encounter groups, is often nothing more than sentimental posturing. Even the anger evoked in these programmed affairs by an aggravated stranger, miffed partner or a facile facilitator is most often little more than a bit of petulance over a peripheral private wound suffered in a childish skirmish and, therefore, not of paramount importance. Unfortunately there is a widespread compulsion today to "feel comfortable" with everyone and everything and to identify that feeling with love or goodness.

But Paul speaks as frequently and as potently of the wrath of God as of the love of God and both in terms of a steadfast and militant realism. This doughty defender of the rights of God does not permit us to wallow in sentimental illusions about God's love, nor delusions of our own lovableness, nor about our harmony with the Creator, creation, or ourselves. We must face the formidable abyss between ourselves and the Wholly Other. We must allow the radical rupture in our relationship with God to be healed. We are by birth, as members of the human race, children of wrath (Eph. 2:11-13); and this wrath sets the stage for the drama of divine love, and is indeed itself a vehicle of that love. This is the human predicament which Paul never forgets. He strongly resists those who do and roars with indignation!

But he is not depressed by the human condition. He knows nothing of Jansenistic rigorism, nor Calvinistic grimness. Nor does he even vainly luxuriate in "high IQ whimpering" à la Sartre. He faces the problems of a recalcitrant human nature, copes victoriously and becomes free. He then unwaveringly proclaims the way to freedom, the way out of the "flesh," the world of endless means, which Nixon naively referred to as "civilization as we know it." Like a thunder clap, Paul expressed the way out of the maelstrom and across the abyss into freedom by pointing to Christ and announcing with wild joy and wonder: "We have a pontiff"; we have a bridge over the gulf between God and man.

Paul rampaged all over the eastern Mediterranean from Antioch, Syria to Rome, Italy, pouring out written and spoken words, worrying the philosophical bones of Greeks and Romans with biblical metaphors, flailing Jewish minds with biblical scorpions. He was an unrelenting gnat on the rump of the world. To be rid of him they finally crucified him upside down on the Appian Way. But not before he had transformed an awful lot of matter in the fire of his spirit, the spirit of Christ in him.

A Married Mystic

Elizabeth of Hungary was born in 1207, in Pressburg. It is said she was "perfect in body, handsome, of a dark complexion." At fourteen she married a childhood friend Louis (Ludwig) of the Thuringian court, at the castle of Wartburg; they were deeply in love. She died in 1231 at the age of twenty-four.

Elizabeth was thoroughly human and completely natural. She was a saint because all her good human stuff was raised to the limit, the utmost possibility of her being. She was—and this is the essence of sanctity—a great lover. She had a generous heart with an incomparable capacity for self-giving. It was the life of the Spirit in her that raised all her naturally good and lively vibrations to a higher dimension, giving them a quality of glory and finality, as it lifted this loving soul into the sphere of Infinite Being. The risk involved was enormous, the love was perilous, the courage demanded was heroic. The sanctification of Elizabeth was as dangerous as an avalanche, sweeping away all the boundaries and landmarks of a well-ordered life and renewing the face of the earth. The base of her whole sanctifying process was her passion—pure eros—the fire of her unbridled, exuberant nature. Her zestful, almost Zorbatic involvement in life has a lucent quality that even the most casual observer cannot overlook.

Elizabeth was a great lover of God and his whole creation. Her passionate devotion to the living God subdued all inordinate desires and addictive human behavior. The fire of God's grace drove out all sloth and indolence. Hers was a soul on fire with the white heat of the mystical life. White heat cannot be contained.

Why shouldn't the blood catch fire from a white-hot soul? It does. That is why, in Elizabeth's case, her spiritual life was among other things, a vibrantly rich emotional life. Elizabeth did not find the love of God incompatible with a real, natural, burning love of a human being. When Louis "took the cross" and went off crusading, she knew the pain of parting, of anguished and unappeasable loneliness.

In her unbounded and vehement love, her grief over the absence of her husband was unreasonable, despairing: screaming and weeping she rushed through the castle like a person demented. She sank into a sea of sorrow, and was submerged beyond rescue in the dark waves of depression. No spiritual ferverinos, pious prattle or friendly stroking could assuage her. Neither could brilliant rationalizations. There was no need, for she was glorifying God by her passionate human feelings, by her erotic flesh and her boiling blood.

In her husband's absence she hungered for his caress; when they dwelt together she expressed her affection for him with a boundless measure of blissful joy. She even demonstrated her emotion publicly with un-self-conscious abandon, kissing him "right heartily with more than a thousand kisses on the mouth!"

This bouncy, sexy Hungarian princess made her husband

happy in the ways that fiercely devoted, playfully saucy wives usually do. She wore her fine clothes on special occasions to celebrate events and to please her husband.

She was not wedded to things. Who, in love, ever is? Ultimately she was married to God alone. Paradoxically, but indubitably, her prince, her spouse, was part of that Alone. After all, God is not one more thing, not even the highest or the best, that replaces another thing. He is the All. As Thomas Merton explains: "The one thing necessary is not that which is left when everything is crossed off, but it is perhaps that which includes and embraces everything else, that which is arrived at when you've added up everything and gone far beyond."[3]

This holy woman was driven by the mightiest power in the world, the love of God: not the love of God in a vacuum, not even the love of God in her head, but God's suprapersonal love intimately in touch with and enflaming, with terrific force, her own untamed nature. She, of course, is ingenuously oblivious of her radiance from the divine fire within, but she suffered from the scorching heat of its purifying flames.

What stands out in the spiritual life of this remarkable woman is her full-bodied, creative participation in life, her own brand of *personal passionate presence*. Look at her care of the sick and poor: a far cry from our sensible and practical welfare work and organized charity. It is passionately personal and intimate, inspired by her love of them as persons and by her own willful determination—however hard and unpleasant—to be her best self. A "best" self is always one that overflows. And so she sought out even the most scurfy lepers. Publicly and secretly she regarded her princessly position with arch tushery, as she took the lowest places and engaged in the meanest and most disgusting services to make others happy.

The words of Mother Teresa, doing "something beautiful for God" today in India, might have been spoken by Elizabeth herself in thirteenth-century Hungary: "Without our suffering, our work would just be social work, very good and helpful, but . . . not part of the Redemption . . . all the desolation of the poor

---

3. Thomas Merton, *Contemplation in a World of Action* (Garden City, N.Y.: Doubleday and Co., 1971), p. 341.

people, not only their material poverty, but their spiritual destitution, must be redeemed, and we must share it, for only by being one with them can we redeem them."[4]

Like Christ who multiplied enough loaves to feed all of China, so moved was he by a hillside of hungry people, Elizabeth cleaned out her palace pantry to feed the hungry townspeople. As does Mother Teresa after her, she gave the poor not only her care but also her heart. She did not merely feed them from her opulent and privileged position, but dressed like them and dwelt with them and shared their poverty—and their freedom from the pomposities and absurdities of the shackled rich. Shortly after her marriage, she rescued a deserted leper and put him in her bridal chamber. Her mother-in-law was horrified; but her husband understood. Her perfection was so relative and right that God's hold on her did not deprive her of charming imperfections and colorful eccentricities!

What a boon it is to find such strong emotions in a saint! If you strip a saint of her feelings you dehumanize the best image and likeness of God available to us. Sweet and vapid froth may characterize dainty men and women, but certainly not a saint. A holy human being is an unparalleled example of wholeness, a well-ordered version of wildness. Such a live person cannot be deprived of the vital force of emotion, a reality that must invest the mind if it is to catch fire and move from mere notions into vital motions of love. When the Lord God of Israel becomes *my* Lord, *my* friend, *my* beloved, then an emotion of high quality, profound depth and creative energy takes hold of me, and I begin to live life fully. The pettiness, coldness, and mediocrity of my former existence now seems bizarre and grotesque.

Only a person of powerful passion commits himself unconditionally to supreme values and thus realizes union with God. Earthly love takes possession of unclaimed territory. That is why a vacuous life is a precarious one. An uncommitted person is bound to be a prey to worldly allurements. Paltry passions give way to the latest fads and fashions, the most popular opinions and the lightest opposition. But if I love God passionately and intense-

---

4. Malcolm Muggeridge, *Something Beautiful for God* (New York: Ballantine Books, 1973), pp. 67 and 68.

ly, then I do not need to draw narrow boundaries round my love
of his creatures. There is no bad love, only bad relationships. You
cannot love too much. Bad relationships are due to insufficient
love, a love that is either diverted or distorted by an inflated or in-
secure ego.

Capacity for love is perhaps the only indispensable natural
foundation for holiness. I must possess the power and impetus,
the wings of the soul, to forget myself for another's sake, to prize
another more than myself, to face fear and pain for another, and
to risk my life. Friendship with God depends on this.

All human friendships depend upon a central Godward dimension. A hundred really good friends cannot take the place of
God; nor can they quench the divine thirst that impels us into
silent and solitary prayer. Elizabeth was a prodigiously active
woman, but her action was the fruit of her contemplation. Every
weak age in the history of the Church is an excessively social and
egregriously horizontal epoch. Why is this? Because people who
are without God are bound to panic and, in their hysteria, to
become extremely important to one another.

The saints had all sorts of defects. But not one of them was
ever apathetic. Have you ever witnessed a suffering enclose a
friend and exclude you? It's almost unbearable. The real lover
will go to any extreme to overcome such exclusion. I read about a
mother who sat on the street for hours every day with her blind
son. She stayed with him in the bright light of a summer day with
her eyes shut so that she might not be better off than he. We all
have done something like that somehow or other in the course of
our lives. When our Saluki dogs were lost in the woods of Nova
Scotia for many wintry days and nights I used to walk for miles
without a flashlight into the wet thickness of the pitch dark
woods, not only in search of them but, even more so, to share
with them their plight.

Elizabeth's whole life was ruled by a compassion far higher
than this: the dynamic effect of an extraordinary convergence between God's passion and hers. The God she loved was not a separate God but a God *pro nobis*, a God in love, incarnate, in history, in process. She found God in the crowned king and in the
village clown. She perceived him most of all and was supremely
enraptured by him in her princely husband. One day at Mass her

gaze fell upon her spouse in his festive array. She was so deeply moved by the beauty of the sight that she forgot she was at Mass until aroused by the bell! There was nothing "soulful" about her brand of Christianity. Too bad D. H. Lawrence and Nietzsche didn't know about her! They would have been less appalled by the sickly, soulful style of Christian living they so roundly and rightly deplored in their writings.

Though there was something noticeably luminous, even ecstatic, about Elizabeth, she was more earthy than ethereal; and not esoteric at all. Creatures attracted and delighted her but did not imprison her. The more she loved God the more she seemed to prize creatures. She never gave in to the pilgrim's temptation which takes two forms. One is to weary of the road and to build prematurely a refuge in the creature for warmth and protection against the troubling immensity of the invisible, the call of eternity. The other is to evade the responsible suffering that a loving participation in the contingent and continually changing human situation demands of us, by turning in childish, petulant spite against all lovely or worldly creatures and all socio-political events as base or contemptible and declaring flight our only salvation.

It was not aloofness or affluence that made Elizabeth noble. She rescued palace life from the officious boredom and tedious trumpery and the extravagant pageantry to which bored and fettered people are prone. Nobility in a human being intensifies his personal response to created goods. Desire and hunger for created happiness is increased because it is the mirror of eternal values. In fact all things become far more valuable to one who has been touched, certainly to one who has been seized, by God. The greedy and lustful are out of touch, and do not know how to adore.

The life of Elizabeth was a passion precisely because it was a challenge: a choice between an abundance of consumer goods and the absolutely consuming God. Through her primal intuitions and humble, attentive attitudes, Elizabeth perceived penetratingly and perseveringly the difference between the light of a thousand candles and the brightness of the sun. Her struggle was between her ego and her higher self, between her petty role as princess and her regnant role as bride of Christ and, therefore, as suffering servant. The human struggle is always with God, his unconditional demands of love, his relentless pursuit, his haunting, heart-breaking summons. If we back away from this central human contest, we who are gamblers and contesters by nature are bound to fabricate another contest, dramatizing and dressing it up with the panache and panoply characteristic of Evel Knievel or Muhammad Ali. If confirmation of this fact be desired, one need only take note of the fanciful forms of demonology prevalent in the history of mankind. The macabre image of an externalized, circumscribed entity of evil called the devil must certainly be one of our most famous defenses against a duel-to-death with God, as well as one of our most blatant projections of personal rapacity and capacious penchant for evil.

It is our goods that demoralize and debilitate us as we get hooked on them. We are so enthralled by the goods of this narrowly limited world that we do not even recognize how merciful and wise God is when he takes away some good before it destroys us. Whatever we have, the commonest and the rarest, is a gift: to be prized, indeed, nurtured and multiplied like the Gospel talents, but never hoarded, and never valued more than the Giver. Creatures are supportive, no doubt. Without them we would cast about convulsively in a howling wilderness. But they cannot sustain and satisfy us forever. That experiential and verifiable fact need not discourage us anymore than it intimidated Elizabeth of Hungary. All we need to know, as she knew with such carefree certainty, is this: when the support of a creature breaks under us, the only abyss we can fall into is the hand of God.

St. Elizabeth did not allow creatures, not even human beings, to become the all-absorbing end of her life. But neither did she treat them as mere means, functional adjuncts of her own self-realization or sanctification. Elizabeth did not love God instead of or in place of man, which happens when the neighbor becomes a casual medium, no longer a person, hardly an object; love "practices" on him, sees him no longer, stays with him no more, goes straight through him like a glass—to God. In this there is a sinister exploitation of the human person who is treated thus as mere thing and degraded to the status of a chance concomitant of God's service. No, as with Elizabeth, the stranger becomes a friend for my Friend's sake; he is not just an instrument or occasion but a personal object of my love. But the ultimate object and motive is my missing Friend. I hear the name by which God calls him. As Mother Teresa again demonstrates: "The difference between them (social workers) and us is that they were doing it for something and we are doing it for somebody. . . . We give it and we do it to God, to Christ, and that's why we try to do it as beautifully as possible."[5]

The glory of God's creation outshines all unworthiness and ugliness. The merely natural man, the ego, is dead: the narrow self who saves his love, chooses its recipient and gives it only to a few. The liberated man raised up by the risen Christ, has come alive; the same human love, and no other, streams from the new God-born self, extravagant, burning, now awake to keenest sensibility; unfettered for the first time, boundlessly free from every barrier of selfish caution, from every parsimonious witholding, bold enough to dare an overflowing tenderness, sowing now with both hands, conscious of inexhaustible risks. No condescension. Agape. Disposed to all, a slave to none. Giving to all, but belonging to none but God.

We are so thwarted by small, narrow and oblique paths. We were secretly pledged long ago by God to hidden laws whose mysterious inexorability our teachers of methods of perfection cannot fathom. Elizabeth of Hungary knew how limited and lackluster all spiritual practices and religious programs are, and how ineffective even highly developed techniques can be. She knew she could not sanctify herself. Her attitude is caught in the striking words of Rilke's *Stundenbuch*: "I weigh and count myself, my God, but Thou has the right to squander me."[6]

---

5. *Ibid.*, p. 114.
6. Rainier Maria Rilke, *Stundenbuch* (The Book of Hours), trans. by A. L. Peck (London: Hogarth Press, 1961), p. 89 (retranslation).

These reflections on Elizabeth of Hungary are based on notes I took years ago on various "lives" of Elizabeth and on old notes on "emotions in the sanctifying process" based on a dialogue with Ida Gorres, who, I am sure, is the one most responsible for my own love of St. Elizabeth and for many of the Elizabethan sentiments expressed in this chapter.

The Passionate Maiden

Joan of Arc was born in 1412 at Domrémy, a little village of Champagne on the bank of the Meuse, and was burnt at the stake at nineteen years of age. Her original trial and verdict were officially made void in 1451. She was canonized 464 years later. Joan of Arc had enough passion to evoke the hero that was locked up in the unconscious soul of France. Through the voices of her "saints" she heard the cries of the living and the dead of that great nation. She took those voices seriously, responded to the challenge and made history. The ramifications of this history reached far beyond French borders. England and subsequently America were profoundly affected. There are historical reasons for saying that we owe our faith to Joan of Arc.

She took the world seriously, loved it, sacrificed herself for it. Through her life of prayer and contemplation she learned her mission, and a purely earthly and worldly one it was: to expel an enemy, free a people from unendurable political misery, and set a rightful king on his throne. There was no spiritual overtone. Like Elizabeth she was faithful to two Kings, the King of Heaven and the King of France. She feared only that in betraying one she would betray the other. Note her passion as she addresses herself to the enemy in the midst of the war:

> King of England, and you, Duke of Bethfort who call yourself regent of the realm of France; William de la Poule, Earl of Suffort, John, Lord of Thelabat and you, Thomas, Lord of Escalles, who call yourselves lieutenants of the said Duke of Bethfort, do right by the King of Heaven to the blood royal: yield to the Maid who is sent of God, the King of Heaven, the keys of all the good towns you have taken and ravaged in France. She has come hither by orders of the King of Heaven to redeem the blood royal; she is ready to make peace if you do right by her and by France, to which you are to do justice and repay what you have seized. And you, archers, room-companions of war, of high birth or of low, who stand before the good town of Orleans, be off in the name of God, to your own country. King of England, if you do not do so, I am leader in war and in whatever place I may find your folk in France I will turn them out willy-nilly, and who will not obey I shall

kill and who will obey I shall spare. Now believe that you can hold aught of the realm of France. No, by God, the Son of Mary! Charles the King shall hold it, the right heir. For God, the King of Heaven wills it so, as the Maid has revealed to him. He will come at last into Paris with a goodly company. If you will not hearken to the words of God by the mouth of the Maid, in whatever place we will find you, we will strike great swings and make such a rough-and-tumble as has not been voiced in France in this thousand years. Then shall we see which has better right from the God of Heaven, we or you. [7]

Joan understood that the misery of her world was rooted in sin. Such distress was not simply "willed by God." Revealed in its lightning flashes of terror and human anguish was the offended will of God, the transgressed law of the Most High. For God had promised that his laws would secure honor, peace and order only so long as they were obeyed. Men mocked at this instruction, destroyed the dikes which God's wisdom had created; and the floods of wickedness flowed in, raging and ruthless. Joan must come to the rescue. The angel tells her nothing but that she, the "daughter of God," must lead the fight for the Father's will against the evil of the world. Joan, this little girl from a Lorraine village, is the chosen one of God, for she herself feels responsible for the sin and fate of her people. She lays the blame nowhere but on her own shoulders and takes her stand before God, asking his command.

Where worldly reality is so dense that seemingly no glimmer of divine light can break through, where opposing forces of evil rise up in all their violent ugliness, there lurks the temptation to despair: to doubt the victory of God's will. There lurks that pilgrim's temptation to assume that certain areas of human life: the political, the social, the economic arena are hopeless, inherently lost, beyond redemption. We feel we must flee this arena to remain untainted; renunciation of the world becomes the sole means of protection from it. If we are "dragged into" it, we will, as part and parcel of it, be delivered to its evil powers, refusing

---

7. H. Belloc, *Joan of Arc* (New York: Declan & McMullen Co., 1949), pp. 33-34.

obedience to God in order to survive. The disorder of the world is incurable, we say; the world cannot be reborn or remodelled. To believe in such possibility is to build castles in the air. We can only create and fortify special enclaves within the world, governed by particular regulations which enable us to follow the will of God alone. The world is doomed to destruction and is hardly worth anybody's bother. Why be concerned? Why sweat it or shed blood in battle for it? Better to confine ourselves to the eternal sphere, the realm of the imperishable or "purely spiritual."

The passionate maid overcame all such temptation. She is in the world, in the midst of its awful vanity, in order to be tested by it. The will of God will indeed fulfill itself in the world; hence the world must be taken with utter seriousness. God is an incarnated God. In the vanity of the world sin is committed and confusion wrought, but there, too, are found fidelity and steadfastness, obedience, confirmation, and redemption. Joan's mission is to subject this mighty vanity, the world, to the will of the Most High God. It is no empty test, no artificial contrivance, no exercise in pure obedience. Laid upon her is a task capable of fulfillment, a genuine opportunity for her to save her people and secure their liberty. But she is charged to try, not to succeed. Ah! There's the crux of it!

Joan's was a supernaturally received mission to be fulfilled by natural means: troops, guns, strategy, gold. No legions of angels were promised her. St. Michael was to advise her, not fight for her. She was not invulnerable to cut or thrust, or immune from mishap or illness. She was a sober saint, a truly peasant woman. There was no romantic air about her behavior. People asked in vain for signs and wonders; she asked for soldiers.

She conquered as she fell, preferring death to adjuration. She conquered, and her funeral pyre, which could not consume her heart, remains a symbol of the utter powerlessness of violence over the soul. She fell, of course, forsaken, conscious of defeat and shame. Else her sacrifice could not be complete; victory must be won at such a price.

In the intensity of Joan's human struggle to stamp the lost and refractory world with the seal of God's will, the question of personal holiness or personal salvation sinks into insignificance. Joan "sought" these only in unconditional surrender to her mission; for her, question of manner and method did not arise.

It is remarkable that in Joan's life as in Elizabeth's, a systematic asceticism plays no part, or at least we are not aware of its doing so. Prayer, of course, is primary. No Christian life, ordinary or extraordinary, is conceivable without prayer. Joan prayed a great deal as a shepherdess with her sheep. Mass was celebrated daily in her camp and daily she received the Body of the Lord. The withdrawal of the sacrament was the worst and most malicious torture of her long martyrdom. Joan was so totally immersed in existence, so unequivocally caught up in a worldly God-centeredness, she did not need to prod and push herself into life with a stiff upper lip. Life itself was her asceticism precisely because she was so passionately alive, so willing to suffer whatever the glory of her nation and her God required of her.

But the question of asceticism as a special way to perfection, as a turning away from the world, a flight from the world, as bodily mortification, did not seem to occur in her life at all. She knew nothing of the great controversy about holy poverty which had occupied minds in ecclesiastical circles for decades. She knew no fear of the things of the world. She loved magnificence and even luxury—fine weapons, clothes, and horses—as naturally as she loved her village simplicity and the rigors of camp. She did not shrink from accepting joyfully silver armor and splendid saddle and harness; she chose costly material for her banner, and bright colors, loving it "forty times more than her sword." During her examination before her persecutors she replied with simple pride to a question about her horse. "Which?" she asked, "for I had four." With unruffled tranquility of spirit she accepted title and coat of arms, presents and privileges. She did not shy away from the excessive enthusiasm and adulation of the people who swarmed about her as she rode into the provincial capital. She had no fear of the splendor of the court with its feasting and mastered its ceremony with untroubled grace. She hated only the noise and roughness of the drinking-bouts! She revelled with the rest in knightly play with steed and lance.

Joan is the maiden with pure and undivided heart, absorbed by a singular passion. But her maidenhood is in no wise hidden from men with veil or enclosure. Her attitude is so unmistakable in its sheer approachability, in its consecrated inviolability, that men never appear in the guise of enemy or danger, but as comrade, brother, friend. The cordiality, the ingenuousness, the graceful freedom of her fraternal attitude towards her soldiers and knights are extraordinary; her faithfulness to the king unexceptionable, utter, passionate. There is never a thought that any of these male relationships might constitute spiritual danger.

Joan of Arc dreams of returning to the arms of her parents, to her forsaken flock, to her spindle by the fireside, and this charms her in the midst of camp life more than all her triumphs. She is a brave and obedient child, lost for the sake of a great love: love of God and of her people, but worked out in the nitty-gritty of her worldly situation. For this reason she is assuredly an inspiration and a saint for our age.[8]

True passion creates the mighty dynamic strength of a Paul, an Elizabeth, or a Joan of Arc, whose energies were all controlled and directed by a lofty ideal. These three inflamed individuals represent the ardent, vibrant tradition of the Church. How did we ever become so uninspired?

The examples used in this chapter to specify concrete instances of Christian passion in person and in action may seem too heroic to be typical. It seems like a good idea therefore to say something about the passionate nature of St. Therese's *Little Way*. This is not a life-style discovered by Therese Martin in France at the turn of the century. It is the Gospel Way discerned by the Little Flower in the Carmel of Lisieux as she struggled with every fiber of her being to surrender unconditionally to the overtures of God's love.

The Little Way

Therese of Lisieux, that young Carmelite nun, an ordinary French girl, brought up in a representative family of a bourgeois society, grasped with unusual perspicacity the general paradox of Christian discipleship: maturity and childhood are somehow iden-

---

8. These reflections on Joan of Arc are based on notes after a lecture by and visit with Cardinal John Wright. They were originally published in *Desert Call*, Winter 1973.

tical. It was Christ himself who made the recovery of childhood the condition of discipleship and of human maturity. Therese, in her *Autobiography* (a spiritual classic that very few "moderns," however hip and au courant, have read), emphasizes this paradoxical identification of maturity and childhood, and shows in a very unshowoffey manner, how this little way is the key to the understanding of prayer and the mystical life.

My own experience as spiritual director of so many people who have come to the desert or to the woods to join our eremitical community but could not make it has led me to the following conclusion. In almost every single case the candidate who left could not survive in the stark simplicity of the contemplative life because in that person the integration of childhood and maturity never took place. I have found this to be equally true in most instances of religious or ecclesiastical defection (excuse the word, but it's a good one). Many divorces are due to the same problem.

Without the dialogue between Jesus and his Father that runs like blood through the life of Christ, we would be forced to interpret his career on this earth as a catastrophe. It is the dialogue that gives positive value and meaning to his life and death. So when his disciples asked him to teach them to pray he simply introduced them into the realm of this child-father dialogue. In order to experience the passionate fatherhood of God, the disciple must become a passionate child. "Unless you become as little children you cannot enter into the kingdom of God."

In order to become wholly attached to God as Father, belonging to him with unconditional childlike trust, one must become detached from, wholesomely independent of one's human parents or any earthly equivalent. This was extremely difficult for Therese, spoiled as she was by her father and an older sister, but she did it, and it was the crucial act that paved the way for her freedom and her sanctification. As Freud made so painfully clear, this liberating step is a difficult one to take. Most parents, even today, exert excessive control and a deadening influence on their children, especially grown-up children, and turn "the family" into a false kingdom of God. Most young people are still inordinately attached to their parents and their parents' world. It is a bit discouraging to reflect on how often the religious life and even the desert experience is spoiled by parental interference and family attachments. It would be salubrious for all of us to meditate more frequently and seriously on the clarity and vehemence with which Christ addressed himself to this subject. His call is so total that once his voice is heard one cannot even "look back."

You cannot turn toward God without turning away from what is not God. You will discover and savor everything all at once in God—later. But first you must make the turn, take the leap. Every true vocation is Zorbatic: "Every man needs a little bit of madness, otherwise he will never cut the rope and be free." You find this madness, this mature childhood in the doctrine and experience of all the great Christian mystics. You will find it also at the creative center of any good spiritual writer.

In trying to describe prayer most of the saints found that the best possible image was a child speaking to his father; and the father is God. And the best possible prayer is the great filial prayer of Christ, the Lord's Prayer, a prayer for all of us, at all times, on any spiritual level. As St. Teresa of Avila points out, indeed as she demonstrates in her own life, the highest degrees of contemplation can be reached in one Our Father well said. Our prayer, even the Lord's Prayer, is no good unless it expresses our own inner truth or what, at least, we most desire to be true. Our lives must be as childlike, ardent, and truthful as our prayer.

I found an insight into this subject that is so stunning I am going to quote a whole page from an article by the distinguished Irish philosopher, Fr. Noel Dermot O'Donoghue, O.C.D., a professor at Edinburgh University.

Essentially the Christian way of childhood is a way of entry into the Trinitarian mystery of fatherhood, filiation and that eternal breathing of love which is the Holy Spirit. The life and death of Jesus of Nazareth is the revelation of eternal childhood in history. The Eucharist is the most complete recapitulation in practical surroundings but now open to all that is, to God and men and all creation. It is a creative involvement in the dynamism of creation. It identifies with creation at the point where all creation is prayer, a response to the God who creates because he loves. It is not easy to achieve, because it demands detachment from the possessive self and from all that is finite and particular, and it is never finally achieved. But it must be emphasized that the detachment is only the negative side; positively what is in question is a deep warmth and tenderness, an all-fathering, all-mothering love, for the child of God shares his father's attitude towards creation. It is in the child as beauty is in the flower; it is only in maturity that a human being can make his own of it, can detach the idea of it and make it a living ideal.

As I see it, the basic dynamism of prayer, especially mystical prayer, is the affectivity of childhood, enlarged, refined and purified through experience. Experience presents us with much that is easy to accept, but it also presents us with the cross, and this is not easy to accept, certainly it is not easy to accept with open arms. Yet it is only insofar as we open our arms to the cross that we can open our arms to the world and that we can open our arms to God in filial love.. It is the cross that extends our affection beyond the particular; in fact the very process of detachment from particular love is no small part of the experience of the cross. Mystical prayer is essentially the expression of a love that has grown beyond the particular by growing through the experience of the love of the particular, especially of particular persons. This love is full of pathos and loneliness, for it is an exile in the world; it is always being misunderstood in its most innocent and spontaneous expressions and manifestations, for the world can only understand love grossly, having lost childhood. It is deeply marked with the sign of the cross; otherwise it is not genuine. Yet if there is any state that may be termed blessed and heavenly it is here it is found, here and in the most perfect days of childhood.

I think it must be admitted that the mystic will always be at odds with the world. There is nothing the worldly man, especially if he be a successful and respected clergyman, judges so quickly and so harshly as the mystical and the mystic, since he has by the very nature of his gift the simplicity of a child and leaves himself wide open to this judgement. Yet I do not despair that the world may change in this matter. Rather, it seems to me, the world will have to change in this, or else one has to despair of the world. For today, for the first time in history man can destroy himself, and there is nothing more certain than that man will destroy himself utterly unless there is a change in the forces within him from which his decisions spring. The balance must shift from the performance principle and all its attendant ambitions and hatreds in favour of the creative principle which has its final basis in the simple, spontaneous, as yet undifferentiated affectivity of the child. This is the way of mystical prayer. It is not a way of our own doing. It is the work of the Spirit of God. Our work is to prepare for his coming. Our prayer is that he may transform our prayer into the eternal love of the Son for the Father. [9]

The spirituality of childhood which dominates the Christian tradition requires no strongman acts, no glittering achievements, no spectacular successes. What it requires is total love that lasts forever. Such a commitment to perfect love may not involve anything big or dramatic at all, but demand instead a passionate fidelity to a hundred little things.

The Child, the Sage, and the Clown

I share the secret of the child, of the saints and sages, as well as of clowns and fools when I realize how wondrous and marvelous it is to carry fuel and draw water. Once the spiritual significance of such ordinary earthy acts dawns on me, I can skip the yoga and koans, the mantras and novenas.

One finds pain and pleasure, ecstasy and enstasy, God and man in the commonplace. All these good natural experiences usher us, if we let them, into the presence of God, into supernatural life. It's better to stay home and smell a flower, bake an apple pie, or sweep the floor than to have a spooky, spurious religious experience at a prayer meeting. It's better to simply enjoy the sunshine or a good show than to meddle curiously and conceitedly with the occult. It's better to romp with the dogs in the back yard than rap with the intellectuals on campus or at church, if the dogs in the yard help us to be less egotistic and more God-centered.

Ordinarily the best contemplative activities are those where contemplation is least emphasized. For instance, self-conscious, highly structured "houses of prayer" are less conducive to contemplation than the average city dump. The higher experiences of the spiritual life are most desirable. But they are most likely to occur if we are at home with and are enjoying the daily things that fill our lives. They provide the only foundation we've got for

---

9. Noel Dermot O'Donoghue, "The Paradox of Prayer," *Doctrine and Life* XXIV (Jan., 1974), pp. 36-37.

skyhigh peak experiences. If there's no foundation, there's nothing. How can we relish the higher things of God if we cannot enjoy some simple little thing like a glass of beer, a boat ride, a hot tub, a good kiss, a belly laugh, walking in the rain, lying in the sun—anything that comes along as a gift from God. The inner truth of these good things is always accessible. If we stay in touch and remain faithful to them, we will be ready when he comes.

But in this age of immense sophistication, vast achievement, and jaded sensibilities, the rediscovery of childhood and consequently the perceptive appreciation of the secret surprise of customary objects is a very rare and precious kind of experience, enjoyed almost exclusively these days by unspoiled children, uncanonized saints, undistinguished sages, and unemployed clowns.

There is among us today a great deal of dissatisfaction. I should hope so! Just below the swinging surface there is a dreadful tedium. But the ways out of our torpor, the ways we have chosen, are extremely limited, limited precisely because they are extreme. In our panic we want to do drastic, frenzied things like getting out of the Church, the Religious Life, the Ministry, or getting off the earth. We want ecstasy, which means quite literally, standing outside, going beyond, being beside oneself. What we want is way up or way out, beyond the regular, repetitive commonplaces of life, like cleaning house or weeding the garden.

It really doesn't matter what type of work we do or what our vocation is, the big illusion is the same: that self-realization and fulfillment lie on some far perimeter of existence to be reached by escaping from and transcending the commonplaces of life. And for those of us who take this desperate route up and out, the prosaic dimensions of life are rendered even more boring. It is a sort of Peeping Tom mysticism that, except for a couple of lucky lusty moments of glee, leaves us thwarted and frustrated all life-long.

Our penchant for the ecstatic has distorted our concept of the sacred. We think of it exclusively as time off or time away and set it up in official opposition to the profane. There are, of course, important aspects of the sacred and they do, indeed, distinguish the holy places and hallowed times from the profane. But such meaningful nuances and proper distinctions do not exhaust the meaning of the sacred. In fact such a rigid demarcation of the sacred extends monstrously the boundaries of the profane and highlights its sphere. The distinction between sacred and profane must be made; but it must also be overcome. This happens when, becoming like little children, we return to the world of simple things and commonplace events with renewed wonder and refined fascination.

We certainly do need Corybantic moments, mountaintop views, serendipities, and periodic forays into unaccustomed space. But even more important is coming back, moving deeply within, centering down and dwelling there. From this ontological point of our being we can enjoy a Christic incarnational view of the universe. The realm of everyday experience will be reaffirmed and reappreciated with our everyday minds. Once God reveals himself in the breaking of bread, there is no need for miracles. If God has spoken and the Word was made flesh, "tongues" are superfluous. Since God has touched man at the core of his being, why care about healing man's extremities?

If we follow the lead of the child, the sage, and the clown we may learn to discover and celebrate the sacred within the profane and respond to divine disclosures in both the squalor and splendor of the world. They are, each in his own unique way, at home with things, seeing the shining insides and detecting all the mysterious connections among creatures. They overcome polarities and reconcile opposites. With their keen insight and cosmic inscape they can feel the tremors and vibrations of the whole earth. This kinship with all that is makes them superbly compassionate. They know what it feels like to be a betrayed man, a lonely woman, a porcupine, a loon, a broken chair, a ripe mushroom, or a steaming mug of coffee.

If children, sages, and clowns sometimes profane holy things, it is in order to reveal the holiness of the profane. The king's crown is handled like an old straw hat while an old match box is guarded like a treasure chest. By means of their naiveté, eccentricity, or buffoonery, they humble the exalted and exalt the humble. Inflated nobility is punctured and lampooned, vulgarity is uncovered and mocked. A thrilling significance is restored to the simplest of things: a penny, a cane, a shy smile, a rakish wink, a pat on the head, or a hop, skip, and a jump. Their lives glow with an extraordinary luminosity amidst the most ordinary circumstances. In a million undreamed of but perfectly natural ways they show how the fat lady, rocking away on her porch, or squeezing onto the subway, is Christ. "Come, let us have a cup of tea" is hardly distinguishable from "Come, follow me." The beauty and majesty of so much driftwood teaches us the same lesson; so do exquisitely artistic creations made of old match sticks and pieces of soap; so do those frames of glory that hang on the walls of Elias, the main house at our Nova Nada Hermitage: dribs and drabs of nature's debris that Tessa found on the forest floor and brought to life again by her imagination, dexterity, and a recreative love.

Unfortunately, we have not been inspired or led by children, sages or clowns. And so we have lost our only possible way into the kingdom of God: the passionate way of childhood, wisdom, and humor. We have behaved more like a chain gang than children of God, as we moved desperately and despairingly from methodological meditation to pharmacological mysticism into charismatic intoxication. Instead of breaking out of our prison the way Paul Newman did in *Cool Hand Luke*, we have smuggled into our enslaved way of life hopeless forms of alleviation and diversion: secular and religious devices and techniques, all sorts of religiosity: from demonology and witchcraft to magic, occultism, and astrology. Progress, bigness, happiness, and novelties of all kinds have been promised us as long as we remain in our prisons.

We can even become incarcerated heroes. But who would not rather be a sane, simple, ordinary human than a manacled hero? We need to become adventurers rather than heroes. Only the adventurer breaks out of the prison and becomes free. Carol Householander once said that the divine architect made the doorway into heaven so small that only children can manage to get through. I would say the same thing about our prison doorways. Only children can get out. Thus the adamant insistence of Christ that we grow up, be reborn, and become as little children. Everything else is prison talk and prison behavior, no matter how eloquent or heroic. Once we are out in the clear we can forget about the high-flying gods and the subterranean demons. We can stop flexing our muscles and revving our engines and abandon all the other ego trips that made prison life bearable. Now we can relax. We are close to earth again. No need for heady Apollonian flights into space, or Dionysian descents into fuliginous darkness. We are already close to God, possessed by God. As mature children a new path has opened up for us, the Little Way, a way of utter simplicity, of ordinary pleasures and commonplace delights.

The following story in the Talmud was particularly cherished by Baal Shem Tov, founder of the Hasidic movement.

Rabbi Beroka used to visit the marketplace where the prophet Elijah often appeared to him. It was believed that he appeared to some saintly men to offer them spiritual guidance.

Once Beroka asked the Prophet, "Is there anyone here who has a share in the world to come?" He replied, "No".

While they were conversing two men passed by, and Elijah remarked, "These two men have a share in the world to come." Rabbi Beroka then approached and asked them, "What is your occupation?" They replied, "We are jesters. When we see men depressed, we cheer them up." [10]

These two men knew the way of the child, the sage, and the clown!

---

10. Quoted by Abraham Heschel, *A Passion for Truth* (New York: Farrar, Straus, and Giroux, 1973), p. 53.

4: Pretty Poison

Our central malaise is not the obvious evil of war, pollution, overpopulation, racism, or crime in the streets. The most destructive force in the world today is a subtle and surreptitious corrosion, a pretty poison that seeps into our best institutions and demoralizes our finest people. Except under close scrutiny and divine illumination, it remains imperceptible. The poison is invisible but enervating; the infection so quiescent that society dies in its sleep.

Pretty poison is the great passion killer, the "corruption of the world's slow stain." After Richard Nixon's downfall he asked a friend: "Are the people going to want to pick the carcass?" No, but it would be a mistake to become complacent about how our democratic American system works, smoking Nixon and his tribe out of office so effectively, without really coming to understand the subtle veins of poison lurking just beneath the surface. We have not yet fathomed the chief cause of our Watergate flood of infections.

> Slowly the poison the whole blood stream fills
> It is not the effort nor the failure tires.
> The waste remains, the waste remains and kills . . .
>
> Not to have fire is to be a skin that shrills.
> The complete fire is death. From partial fires
> The waste remains, the waste remains and kills.[1]

The waste that accumulates and poisons the blood stream is that remnant of our life which we willfully withhold from the transforming fire. Once you recognize how tolerant we have become to this pervasive pretty poison, you begin to realize why death, as the ultimate breakthrough and openness of our life,

---

1. William Empson, "Missing Dates," from *A Map of Modern English Verse*, ed. by John Press (New York: Oxford University Press, 1969), p. 213.

must involve a kind of violence—a wild human passion—if our proud self-imprisonment is to be broken open.

It is the very prettiness of the poison which seductively keeps us safely distanced from the malevolent source of infection. This is best illustrated by an examination of the damaging taming of our passion by the pretty poison of Erich Segal's *Love Story* and Catholic Pentecostalism. And one is as current as the other. *Love Story* as a movie or a book is old hat. But the putrescence in the story and in America's reaction to it goes on. It is that virulent tumor at the core of our society that must be cauterized. But first it must be seen. For that we need a spotlight. For that purpose *Love Story* is as useful as ever.

If I am to be true to the prophetic charism of the Judaic-Christian tradition then I must not follow the revolutionary trend of today, which is to attack capitalism, racism, and imperialism. My diagnosis must go much deeper than that. Shallow thinking has led to the assumption that if we replace capitalism with socialism we will eradicate racism and imperialism. This false assumption has, in turn, issued in noisy and nugatory revolutionary activities. Shifting from one political system or party to another, from one ideology to another does not deliver us from evil. Achieving political ends by political means is an illusion. Anyone who knows Christ knows that. Our efforts must be far more radical than politics can possibly be. We must free ourselves from the binding and blinding forces of *technique* and then detect and describe the focus of infection at the heart of the human predicament.

To do this, to be this critical, is an obligation of love. It is also a difficult and onerous duty. But it cannot be shirked. That is why I consider this chapter to be, though necessarily somewhat negative, the most important part of this book. There can be no integration, no wholesomeness unless negativity is encountered and embraced. We cannot expect virtue of sinners until we recognize the sins of the just. Once we perceive what is wrong with our best men and finest movements—our representatives—then we will know what is really wrong with our society.

That is what I seek to accomplish here. My *loving* criticism of whatever is a criticism of us. I may be the most guilty. But the question must be asked: What is wrong with our most popular concept of love and our most common use of language? I find the clue in Erich Segal and Erica Jong. What is wrong with religion in America? How does the spirit of Christ—the holy Spirit—transform the individual person and whole societies? A critical look at Pentecostalism may provide the best possible way to begin to answer those crucial questions. If the response to this criticism is the customary caveman yawp we have gotten nowhere; if it is a thoughtful, loving rejoinder, however strong and acerbic, we are on our way to the truth.

Love Story Tepidity

Vincent Canby of the *New York Times* called *Love Story* "a first-rate example of a second-rate genre," which means that the story is false tenfold over to love, death, and other human values. But, of course, the genre of the "weepie" has never achieved high standards. Of Segal's sequel, *Oliver's Story*, Christopher Lehmann-Haupt of the *New York Times* wrote: (It is) "so unrepresentative of anything real or recognizable that it is impossible for a reader to work up the faintest interest."

Erich Segal taught Classics and Comparative Literature at Yale. That is incredible in light of the fact that there is absolutely no classical dimension and no literary quality in his *Love Story*, for so long the nation's best seller, and a movie that enthralled almost everyone. There is not an uplifting paragraph in the whole book. Segal is clever but witless. If there is wit, it is a petty, self-conscious wit; certainly there is no notable joviality, no deep exploration, no luminous insight, no serendipities, no corybantics. Can love be so dreary?

Love Story in cinematic form is no better; simply more subtle. You drink in the prettiness more rapaciously, absorbing and assimilating it through all the senses, while the poison sickens you. You lose your mental acuity and succumb to a comatose allurement—a meretricious romanticisim for unremarkable routine lives—and most of us give in.

Segal's *Love Story* is, as such, a spectacular failure. But as a portrait of the death rattle of our declining culture, it is a smashing success. Love story—no. Success story—boy makes it without dad's help—yes. But more people die from success than cancer. The author tries to be another Salinger. A futile attempt, for he has none of Salinger's mystical moods, profound puzzlement, satirical bite. The only thing *Love Story* has in common with *Catcher in the Rye* is uncouth words; but unlike Salinger, Segal uses them ineptly.

I cried toward the end of the book as I was supposed to but for a different reason: even death was banalized by commonplace vulgarity. Poor Jennifer—she lived and died without passion or hope; Oliver was dead from the beginning. Jen married a dead man, but she loved his athletic body. And they spoke the same language, the language of death: "shit," symbol of the desecration of man; and "goddamit," the desecration of Yahweh; and "sonovabitch," the ludicrous belittlement of everything. Sadly and significantly, this is also the language of Watergate and of the former President of the U.S., spoken at crucial meetings in the White House. Watergate, of course, is a superexample of pretty poison.

I wept, too, over the bovine nature of the death scene—brusque and unspiritual. It had to be such, of course. The end of the matter. Sheer guts. What else? There was no effusion of spirit, not even a glint, in the whole love story. Why should there be now? No depths either. A surface struggle—the typical, common, soapbox variety of corny solutions: silly evasions and bogus confrontations: but with a notable difference from the old style: it's all said with dirty words.

The death did relieve the relentless boredom of the story. For such a small book it was a large bore. The death relieved me, too, because otherwise Jen and Oli might have satisfied their desire for another big football or hockey player—and would that diminish our population problem?

The most popular and unfortunately successful technique of the latest breed of authors and playwrights is to fill a pretty-girl mouth, or a sacred moment, or a solemn scene with either foul, obscene words or putrid actions. It's still a novelty to the average reader, and so outrageously inane books still sell. Indeed, such frivolous, salacious stuff dominates the best seller list.

Is there not a sense of pride in the fact that now, for the first time in our history, we may without immunity, without fear or embarrassment, without losing respectability, without guilt, take God's name in vain? "Thou shalt not take the name of the Lord thy God in vain" (Ex. 20:7). Yet we do so a hundred times a day. The nicest people do. It's our biggest sin: our endless effort to tame God, to make him bearable, manageable, useful. And so we try, foolishly, to be casual about God. Mouthing his holy name, instead of standing with fear and trembling in the awesome mystery of the Almighty who reveals himself through his name. We blaspheme in our effort to be autonomous; and we trip ourselves up in our pride.

Every contemplative critic of our society recognizes the ludicrous and blasphemous nature of this pride. And every sociologist worth his salt sees the decay and the desolation that are a direct consequence of our pride and our preening profanations. We wallow with morose delectation in our despair and have found no way of coping with our chaos except as aesthetes who refuse to face reality, victims who are merely carried away by the onslaught of evil, or aggressors who choose to inflict death on others, thereby joining the chaotic masses engaged in the raging struggle to dominate, exploit, and possess.

Our language betrays us. We will understand ourselves only if we come to fathom our own language. We use words cheaply, and to the extent that we do, we abandon our depths and forfeit our dignity. Words are repositories of the spirit. They are pregnant with the spirit the way the body is, but more directly, openly, explicitly, with tangible poignancy.

Once we loosen our words from the ground of our being, detach them from our deep, spiritual source, they cease to be the fruit of the spirit, of loving awareness, and become clichés, garbage in the background of intelligence. We live in a loquacious age: nothing more familiar, more trite than words. We bury ourselves in a veritable Vesuvius of monologue and can hardly escape the insensitive garrulousness of our friends. Words have become the object of frequent and ferocious defilement.

We know from the wisdom of the ages that the defilement of words is the worst kind of corruption. And from the Scriptures, as well as our own experience, we know that "what fills the heart overflows through the mouth" (Mt. 12:34). The kinds of words we use indicate with unfailing precision who and where we are, individually and collectively. Our present, public, unabashed use of profanities and obscenities anywhere, anytime, and in the presence of anyone—child, woman, or holy man—is one of the infallible signs of our corrupt society.

The kids swear away and think they are big brave rebels.

The girls confuse libidinous bluntness with liberation. The brazen talkers are always empty-headed. It's sheer compensation: if there's nothing in the inside, then stir it up on the outside; there's nothing like a loud, labial, and incessant cacophony for a good cover—a compulsive but ineffective camouflage. Far from being rebellious, the dirty-mouthed are actually beastly conformists. They must be. Their lazy language is a dead giveaway. Every petty, herdy, crowdy adolescent talks the same way.

Let me save the defensive reader a uselsss argument. I have not been granted a sheltered life. I have worked in every state except Alaska with every kind of human person and I have taken pains to mingle in an unidentifiable way with all sorts of people. The young are not the only offenders. Adults are just as bad and priests, I am sorry to say, are often worse.

Exposure to bad language is no reason for its tolerance or adoption. To excuse it is to be thoughtless, spineless, and apelike. The most frequent and pointless argument that I run into is: "But this is the way it is; this is reality." Yes, I know. And so is murder, rape, and robbery. Blatant evil, these; but in the long run, perhaps no more destructive than the pretty poison that gradually kills the spirit of a nation by the corrosion of its language.

We live in words, feel in them, think in them, but when we fail to respect their objective dignity, their power and their weight, they turn to dust and ashes in our mouths. Abused words avenge the abuser. Soul and word interact upon one another. The word is a powerful force. We need to climb inside of a word and abide there in love and awe before we can discover the inner richness of person. If our words are profane, vulgar, and violent then one person has been assaulted by another: a brutal affliction far worse than bodily injury or even death.

Of course we are stuck in the twentieth century. Other centuries, like the early Greek and Elizabethan, reverberated with a rich and reverent love-language. Our century is prosaic, a pale reflection of what H. L. Mencken calls "the bland barbarism of the booboisie." We are absolutely eloquent about war, sports, and the products we sell. About love we are amazingly inarticulate. Our language reflects our assertive, utilitarian, exploitative way of life: we no longer engage in the exquisitely delicate, prolonged and ecstatic artistry of "making love," we just matter of factly "have sex"; we don't thoughtfully enter into "intercourse," that profound and purifying process, we "screw" or "ball" a "chick"; we don't "go to bed," a phrase connoting holy leisure and wise passiveness, we "lay" someone else or get "laid" ourselves. This deplorable impoverishment of our language and our love is celebrated in our best selling pseudo-love stories from Erich Segal and Erica Jong and cavalierly and complacently conceded by bourgeois society.

"Well, you can't say it wasn't a relevant rebellion." Why not? If *Love Story* were a rebellion against religion it might have been a worthwhile and timely criticism because so many of us tend to reify religion, turning it into a cozy thing and belonging to it instead of to God. But *Love Story* is a rebellion against religiousness, that is, against man. If you scrap religiousness, which is the deepest thrust of man, you scuttle humanity.

Notice the fact that there were no hallowed moments or events—and no in-depth (or God) experiences. Everything was leveled and done blithely on the surface. Mystery was destroyed. Remember Jennifer directing the boys' choir in church at Christmastime? It was a solemn function in a holy place and with little boys, innocent, fragile, and impressionable. Not spectacularly at all, but tritely, Jennifer desacralized the whole event and thus perverted it, and the boys, God, and all the rest of us by saying to one of the singers: "Don't bullshit me, Paul." The corruption of the best things is the worst kind of corruption. "Woe unto you if you scandalize one of these little ones" (Mt. 18:6-7).

Jen and Oliver skipped the beginnings and so came to an abrupt and absurd end. Can you imagine any real lover saying to the beloved three minutes before dying: "Get the hell out of here; I don't want you at my G--d--- death bed"? They never had and never developed a taste for the right things. The Latin word for that kind of ordered or illuminated tasting is *sapientia* from *sapere*—to taste. The English word is wisdom. And "the beginning of wisdom is fear" (Pr. 1:7, Sir. 1:14). There is no other way into wisdom. You cannot skip wonder and awe, a holy, filial fear. If you do, you may end up crafty and clever, like the *Love Story* mannikins, but certainly not wise. If there is no manful, unruffled fear there is no reverence. And reverence or respect, from *respicere*, which means to take a long loving look at the other, is a key virtue. I'd dare say it's the keyest of all virtues. (Virtue, remember, means the easy ability to act humanly.) Without reverence there is no love. Obviously, there is not an ounce of reverence in *Love Story*—not between Jen and Oliver and certainly not between either one of them and their parents. Oliver clung tenaciously in hateful relation to his father and Jennifer manipulated her father by a cunning relationship.

Rebellion is in order. Quiet, tranquil rebels are in demand. But rebellion without reverence is narcissistic nonsense, a barren stentorian stance. Oliver and Jennifer were thoroughly narcissistic: totally and exclusively immersed in their own perfectly private success story. No social concern, no compassion for others, no broad perspectives, and above all, no compunction. They were not only solipsistic together, and therefore unrelated to the real world; but their solipsism isolated them from each other—hence their favorite slogan: "Love means never having to say you're sorry." Sheer balderdash! Love really means being profoundly sorry forever that you cannot be enough or do enough for the beloved.

Who doesn't know that the most heroic acts of love whether in history, literature, or our own experience of life, have been, not the ebullient blandishments of effusive, turned-on lovers, nor the excessive tolerance of Segal's or Jong's puppets, but rather the prodigal moments of mercy, the altruistic expressions of forgiveness, the staggering humiliation and shame that come with the unbearable recognition that one has hurt the beloved and then the supreme human act of sorrow full of healing, renewal, and selfless adoration? On the religious level, man reaches the pinnacle of all human achievements when with compunction he enters into the abyss of his own nothingness, experiences at the core of his being his own spiritual bankruptcy, grasps existentially and acknowledges humbly his need for a savior, and cries out of the depth of love: "I have sinned, I am sorry. Save me or I perish!"

Consequently there are no sublime moments in Segal-Jong literature, no extremities, no tragedies. Jennifer kept mediocrity alive in *Love Story* from beginning to end and did not create the spark that might have brought Oliver to life. Absolutely everything—even death—was "ok;" not great, not bad, but ok. "I'm an ok musician;" "I look ok for a Thursday night." An ok love story is no love story at all. Love is the most dangerous thing in the world. It jeopardizes your safety, threatens your security and turns your life inside out. It kills your self-constructed little ego, but makes it possible for you to rise up a free man—free for universal, cosmic love, which is the most noble but also the most exhausting human virtue.

People say in defense of Segal's hoax: "But what a lovely laudable switch from pornography and all that sex." Tommyrot! Pornography is far less noxious than Segal's kind of pretty poison. Sex without love is a bore, but so is love without sex.[2] What is missed above all in *Love Story* is eros, that creative source of all kinds of greatness: sexual, social, artistic, religious. The author's story is characterized not by major vices but by minor virtues. And the latter are far more dehumanizing than the former.

This great spoof on the American public is of course not all Segal's fault. While he did not expect to write a classic in three weeks, the masses acclaimed it as the love story of the age. Such a delusion is inevitable in view of our desolate experience of love.

Love Story is a cool story. Segal tries hard to be hip: "lissen" to him. If only he had the power to transfigure matter with spirit, his story would have been touched and saved by love, if not transformed.

I cry at movies. *Love Story* left me cold and dry: it was so obviously unreal, unnatural, artificial. It gulled a lot of people and, worse, a lot of people gulled themselves. They made themselves believe that Segal was indeed telling it like it is, and that's the way it really happens. There was just enough spurious semblance of reality to catch the unwary off guard and make Segal's tale less resistible; and so, inevitably, the strident majority got sucked into the sorcery of Segal-Hiller-Lai and the smirky silliness of O'Neal and MacGraw.

Segal and company worked on our capacity to delude ourselves. There is scarcely a character or situation or a line in the story that rings true, that even approximates real simplicity or generosity of feeling, a sentiment or emotion honestly experienced and expressed. The hoax has become alarmingly unfunny because of the pernicious implications.

---

2. By sex I do not mean genitality, not even sensuality; but rather sexuality which tones up the personal act of love and keeps it from freezing to death.

Why does Jong's majestic trivia attract so many readers? Why does Segal's simpering sob story look like love to so many people? Why does this crisp casual way of being maudlin have such mob appeal? Because of the barren, feeble, and false experience of love granted to most of us as we hobble through life, letting anything happen, moving from distraction to distraction, seeking diversions, driven by our appetites. And while we play along the side of the road and dabble safely in myopia, the real adventure—love—escapes us. And by that I mean any kind of *real* love: a productive, reverent, unifying action of the *whole mind.* I also mean the love that lies beyond and pervades every other love, a total love which alone can free and fulfill at once all human striving.

The whole mind: there's the rub. It's got to be disciplined or illumined love, an exercise of the integral mind in touch with the real. Otherwise, it's a vacuous pseudo-love. And that's our plight. We are in touch with only one-third of reality (the surface dimensions), with one-third of our minds.

We have lost our capacity for the intellectual act—not a cerebral act, but the penetrating venture of the whole mind into the inner core of reality, into "the dearest freshness deep down things."[3] So all our talk about love is babble and our excursions into love are misadventures: a dull, dreary round of events that seem to fill the yawning vacuum of a cellophane age. This trifling passion we call love: it has become our mass cultural bromide. We consume it hungrily and *let ourselves live*, which is the worst and most common form of suicide. No creative pluck, no existential freedom, no moral responsibility. That's why Henry David Thoreau said: "Most men live lives of quiet desperation."

Out of desperation the masses settle for crumbs: *Love Story* and *Fear of Flying*, for instance, in one case a smarmy, anachronistic regressive piece of idealization; and in the other a boot camp exhibition of female sexual aggression.

Jong's chronicle of Isadora's sexual exploits, including a good many scatological references, is at least as loveless and unin-

---

3. Gerard Manley Hopkins, *Poems and Prose*, ed. by W. H. Gardner (Baltimore: Penguin Books, 1963).

teresting as Segal's earlier story. I was persuaded to read *Fear of Flying* by Jong's new fan, Henry Miller, who sees her as the new intellectual woman novelist. The author of *Tropic of Cancer* must be miserable, longing for company in his socio-sexual wasteland, because Jong never takes off (despite all the unzipping) and comes nowhere near achieving a high quality piece of prose. The book is poorly constructed, has a shapeless plot and a bunch of weak characterizations. What little identity Jong's heroine enjoys she derives from her relationship with men. Her tiresome account of these besotted relationships has caught the imagination of the populace. Her hardcover has sold 50,000 copies and her paperback, presently in the eleventh printing, has sold over 1.5 million copies.

Jong and Segal are so easy to read! No effort, no mystery or challenge, no muscular intellectual work, nothing new, and nothing so old yet so durable that it's still a good read or worth a trip to the theatre. People gobbled up *Love Story* despite the clumsy, awkward writing, such as: "I ambled over to the reserve desk to get one of the tomes that would bail me out on the morrow." At that reserve desk occurs the fatal meeting and, forever after, the phony dialogue which doesn't peter out until Jennifer does—which should be noted as the most palling and empty dialogue in the history of literature and filmdom. It is monumental kitsch, schmaltz, and unrelenting chatter. There's no reason why this movie should not have ruined Ali MacGraw's career. She plays her role as superciliously as her worst lines read. She does nothing but bully Oliver with her boorish, brazen tongue which is meant to be groovy. That's why she never takes that smug expression off her face. Ali would have killed the movie, but alas, the proneness of viewers to identify with her as heroine proved to be the stronger.

There is one thing, though, that Ali catches from Segal and painfully conveys to the rest of us: Egotism and a stupefying want of compassion. We always have known that there is only one power that destroys love: selfishness. Now all the insufferable egotists who have been reading and watching *Love Story* can say with a self-satisifed smirk: so we are lovers after all.

And, after all, isn't that the American way? Anyone can be president—and how!—anyone can be a lover—no way!

The Catholic Pentecostal Teacup

Far from being either an appropriate response to or a rejection of divine passion, Pentecostalism seems more like a diversionary tactic. It is a school of mediocrity that teaches us how to get close to the fire of God's pure passion without getting burnt. The trick is to get just close enough to be warmed by the fire. That's lukewarmness.

It is imperative to take Pentecostals seriously. I do. I love and respect every one of them. Out of this love has grown my concern, my worry and finally, after eight attentive, anxious years, my criticism. It is not a criticism of mainline Protestant Pentecostalism. My use of the word Pentecostalism is, in every case, a reference to the Neo-Catholic version. I cannot call the movement "charismatic." That's a good, strong word, and I hate to see it spoiled.[4]

It is equally important to take seriously the whole phenomenon of Pentecostalism because it is a subtle but salient sign of a human drought, of a people who, for a very long time now, have been starving to death on weak rations of rationalism. The signals should be recognized and the problems attended to; but then the whole phenomenon should become a pointer or stepping stone that helps lead us into the mystery, into the fire.

Into the mystery, where "the eye with which I see God is the eye through which he sees me," where his Cry is my cry, where Creator and creature, Lover and beloved are drenched in the same naked essence. This is baptism of the Spirit. Fullness of being, sacred silence, soul-full solitude. Anything else would be disgusting: placebos, platitudes, the frenetic banter of inane testimonies, or the sanctimonious "praise God" drivel that some of us resort to so carelessly.

What does God abominate? It has been revealed: prayer,

---

4. Since I am merely using Pentecostalism here as an example of pretty poison, I cannot now defend my position with irrefutable arguments. I do so in *Pentecostal Fire*, a more formal and extended version of this criticism (a discriminating fusion of censure and eulogy), based on eight years of research and experience. This is currently in preparation with the assistance of my co-worker, Patricia McGowan, and my coauthor Tessa Bielecki. We look forward to publication in 1978.

when words predominate. "I hate, I despise your feasts, and I take no delight in your solemn assemblies. . . . Take away from me the noise of your songs; to the melody of your harps I will not listen" (Amos 5:21, 23-24). For several years I have attended many different Pentecostal prayer meetings. If therapy was their purpose, some of them were fairly good. If prayer was their purpose, they were an abomination: a degradation of man and a banalization of God through a distortion of prayer.

Be slow to pray. There is no other approach to God. It is a terrible thing to get caught up in the hands of the living God. Be sure to pray; "pray without ceasing" (1 Thessalonians 5:17). But be slow to pray. "Be still and see that I am God" (Ps. 46:10). What is asked of us by the Psalmist is God-consciousness, not prayer-consciousness. Prayer-conscious people are likely to be pious prigs. God-conscious people *seem* like atheists because their faith is so pure. Pure, too, is the God they know so obscurely. They can find no image, no concept to do the utterly Mysterious One justice. Nikos Kazantzakis said of prayer: "When I pronounce a word, for instance, Lord, this word shatters my heart. I am terror stricken and do not know if I shall be able to make the leap to the following words: Have pity on me."[5]

Nikos reminds me of St. Teresa of Avila. How often she began the Our Father and never got any further than those first two words! Intuitively overwhelmed by her own existential filiation, her own intimate participation in the Godhead, she was stunned into an abyss of stillness, into silent, solitary adoration.

Teresa, in turn, reminds me of any decent lover at home in the art of love-making, or any real friend enjoying a really good get-together. Testimonials would be out of place. Can you imagine lovers and friends getting up and seriously saying something like: "I came to testify that my beloved or my friend, Sarah, came to my rescue three times last week when I was hungry, lonely, or in some kind of trouble; and that's why I'm here"? You'd never say anything like that in the house of your beloved or your friend! How much more foolish the situation becomes if once the testimonial is over and done with, all the other friends start chirping:

5. Nikos Kazantzakis, *Report to Greco* (New York: Simon and Schuster, 1965), p. 88.

"Praise Sarah! Praise Sarah!" Along with a whole chorus of mumbo-jumbo in Sarah's honor. Of course, it's a very strange thing in the first place that there is a bunch of people in on this love-making session or this intimate encounter between friends. But that's one of the odd things about "prayer groups."

In the fire, tongues are cleansed with burning coals and thus speak with clarity and authority. But there is no fire, no clarity, no authority in what today, as in other effete ages of the Church, is presumptuously called "the gift of tongues"; it is a ghastly form of bedlam. Far from being a gift, it is both for the community and for the person a rift.

The "tongues" we hear babbling today at prayer meetings all over the country are nothing like the tongues of the original Pentecost—the only authentic instance of tongues that we know of in the whole history of the Church. The reasons for and effects of that singular instance of tongues were exactly the opposite of today. Anyone who wants the so-called gift of tongues, who strives for it, or claims possession of it, cannot possibly have known the experience of prayer.

It's hard to imagine how we ever got so outlandishly sidetracked. I think we have suffered enormously ever since we gave up the *Imitation of Christ* and the *Lives of the Saints.* We need to keep our eyes on Christ and follow the Christian pattern of the saints—especially the big ones. I mean people like Mary and Joseph. They are as imitable as they are admirable. It's hard to imagine their having chummy rap sessions with or about Jesus. And if they did wonders, we know nothing about them. So the least we can say is that the Evangelists did not think them relevant enough to mention.

All of the Apostles were mystics but none of them was a charismatic, at least, not in the debased sense of the word bandied about today. And Paul, who seemed a bit mad himself, was embarrassed by the queer behavior of the Corinthians. All the crazies were gathered in Corinth, and Paul had to come to terms with them. So he settled for a less evil situation. The gist of what he had to say to them was this: If you must, you must; but please, do your woeful whimpering and whining, your joyful cackling in the privacy of your homes. Reserve the church for real prayer (cf. 1 Cor. 14). Although there's no evidence of Paul ever speaking in tongues, wisely—a good public relations technique—he let on that he had the gift himself. But there's no evidence the Corinthians ever heard him babbling.

I suspect that Paul's gift was very much like my own, a gift I've enjoyed for many years. It's a weird kind of gibberish I sometimes resort to in private dialogue with God or myself, or in the heat of a volley ball game. Every once in a while it pops up in the middle of a Mass or a sermon. Both my listeners and I know it's ridiculously funny and blatantly out of place, so we laugh! Apart from sonorously expressed songs and well-delivered speeches I've heard, that's the only gift of tongues I know about—except Pentecost.

Among Pentecostals, glossolalia is already fading. The spectacular but short-lived quality of this sputtering and sporadic phenomenon is characteristic of its nature and history in the Church. Pentecostals have turned now to healing. Unlike tongues, faith healing really happens; I should hope so! It would be a sad world without daily miracles. I witness at least six or seven a day. They keep me going and make me glad to be alive. To witness to and participate in divine pathos, the healing, saving mercy of God, which is his favorite daily miracle, is one thing. To stage miracles is another. Miraculous performances are detestable, unless they are essential and spontaneous.

Christ performed miracles reluctantly, and whenever possible, secretly. He exerted this kind of power only in desperate situations, in condescension to human weakness and human blindness. As he grew in grace and wisdom, and his followers grew with him and were more willing and able to live by the hidden power of his spirit, there were notably fewer miracles. After the Resurrection and the promulgation of it, culminating in Pentecost, there was hardly any need for miracles at all.

The only miracle Jesus seemed to really care about was *metanoia*, a radical change of mind and heart. What good is bodily healing if there is no transformation of character, no integration of the personality?

"Prayer is the only miracle. We pray. When our words become prayer God comes."[6] That is why the saints very seldom heal bodies miraculously. That is why their own bodies are so

---

6. Brian Moore, *Catholics* (New York: Holt, Rinehart and Winston, 1972), p. 107.

often in such bad shape. They live so vigorously and love so recklessly, their bodies can't stand the strain; neither, in some cases, can their nerves. You can tell by their scarred bodies that they really suffer life with all they have, "filling up what is wanting to the passion of Christ" (Col. 1:24). This is not only true of the canonized saints of the past. It is true of most of the living saints I know right now.

I do not agree with the most common criticism of Pentecostalism, namely, that it is too emotional. My basic contention is just the opposite: it is not emotional enough. It is, in fact, almost devoid of any real fervor. Fervor is the contrary of lukewarmness, and therefore it always means a profound dissatisfaction with our own state. It means you want to want God and want to want nothing else. The average Pentecostal wants tongues, healings, prophecies, and a good religious experience every week, if not every time he prays.

What these prayer groups often lack is powerful passion—tough, towering emotions. This is certainly my own observation but not, by any means, my unique critical contribution. As we point out in *Pentecostal Fire*, those who know the most about worldwide Pentecostalism from within and without—for instance, Walter Hollenweger[7]—do agree that the salient weakness of the Neo-Catholic American brand is precisely its pathetically weak emotional dimension.

The Pentecostal testimonies are invariably insignificant as well as insipid. In tongues, words are not only mangled but mincing. If they cannot be lucid at least they can shriek like hungry birds until their throats tear into a thousand pieces! Prophecies are nothing more than the puffings of bloated egos. The hymn singing is often dull. The cross is conspicuous by its absence. So is the broken world.

The effect of these religious jamborees is usually the same: God has been had, Christ has been tamed, the Spirit has been corralled. Or so Pentecostals surmise! These are not the words they use. They speak triumphantly of a "baptism of the Spirit."

---

7. Walter Hollenweger, *Pentecostals: The Charismatic Movement in the Churches*, trans. by R. A. Wilson (Minneapolis: Augsburg Publishing House, 1972).

You are not really a member until you are baptized in the Spirit. How do you know? There are two signs. One is external and unmistakable: you speak in tongues. The other is internal and usually threefold: a nice warm feeling for Jesus, other members, and yourself; a pitiful concern for those outside; and a growing excitement about praying together. Together almost always means holding hands and saying something really "neat" as if to God, but really to one another for comfort, solace or edification; or else, everyone simultaneously mumbles or sings something audible but unintelligible that leaves the group swinging, swaying, and sweating in blissful camaradarie.

Is this religious renewal? Is this the life of the Spirit, the wild and uncontainable Spirit of God whose breath creates and sustains the universe, a universe that would disintegrate without that vital force seething and swirling inexhaustibly and inexorably toward the Omega Point?

One of my readers is bound to say: "So it's just not your cup of tea." And my stout rejoinder to that is: it's no one's cup of tea precisely because the Almighty God will not be contained in a tea cup. Pentecostalism is a tea cup. That is why it is hard for me to take all the ponderous articles and books on Pentecostalism very seriously. I have had to force myself to do so. All this monumental fuss—theological, psychological, exegetical—over the shape, size, and weight of the tea cup! As if any cup would be a fitting vessel for the triune tidal wave of God's unbearable and infinite reality! It would be easier for a tea cup to contain Niagara Falls than for Pentecostalism to cope with the awful love of God! Pentecostals try to recapture the form but not the ferocity of the original Pentecostal outpouring. They try to reproduce the accidental features without the substance of Pentecost. It's incredible how regularly we head for the shallows and avoid the deeps.

Something like the following fictitious example is what happens. The Smith family is sitting in their Los Angeles backyard, except for Steve who is inside listening to the radio. He hears an astounding announcement, a warning that a devastating bomb will soon be dropped on the city of Los Angeles, and that all residents must evacuate at once according to directions. Steve dashes out into the yard with the news. The folks are indeed startled but somehow get into a discussion about Steve: the way he banged the back door, shouted the news and left the screen door open. This of course delays their departure and endangers their lives. Now Mr. Smith remembers an account of a Japanese evacuation under similar circumstances, except that in the Japanese incident the bomb had already been dropped and the people were scorched and burned in varying degrees as they fled the city. He recalls that the people jumped into the first body of water they reached, screaming and crying at the top of their lungs, many deliberately or dementedly drowning. So the Smiths run a few blocks from home to a body of water owned and operated by the L.A. Sewage Department.

No bomb had yet fallen on the city. It turned out that it never did. But the Smiths felt strongly that they should do what the Japanese did. So they jumped into the water, yelling and whooping like crazy. Within an hour a thousand people were carrying on hysterically in that body of water, some drowning themselves. Police and sewage officials arrived on the scene and tried to get some explanation for this bizarre human behavior. The people in the water were still hooting and hollering, but they seemed almost jubilant now, shouting over and over again: "It's a new Hiroshima! A new Hiroshima!"

This became a very popular religious practice. There were no explosions and never any fire, but thousands of people returned week after week to all kinds of Los Angeles watering holes and did all sorts of foolish things as if they were bombed and burning, yelling festively and triumphantly: "A new Hiroshima!"

Now there may indeed be a new Pentecost stirring in the world of today, a new, fresh burst of Spirit enlivening the Body of Christ. There are smoke signals (signs of transcendence) that indicate that there is a fire blazing somewhere. Where? In all the Pentecostal prayer meetings I have attended in all parts of the country there has been a lot of commotion similar to the antics of the L.A. people celebrating a new Hiroshima, but no fire. I came out of a prayer meeting one day, as offended and tormented as ever. I went across the street into a dingy and decrepit-looking barroom and, there, was restored by the palpable presence of God, who tends to reveal himself in the most unlikely, ungodly places. Maybe I'm not pious enough. I know that even after a long period of normal retreats for normal people, I seem to need the restoration I find on slum porches, the Bowery curbstones, children's playgrounds, railroad tracks, shipyards, and wild beaches.

Perhaps the least hopeful place in all the world of ever finding Pentecostal fire is at a Pentecostal convention. The busyness and crowdedness of a Pentecostal convention are bound to be an impediment and an insult to the *Pure Passionate Presence*; and that's what I mean—as do the Scriptures and the mystics—by Pentecostal fire.

The first Pentecostal who suggested a convention didn't know what he was talking about any more than Peter did when he suggested, after Christ's transfiguration, that they build some tents to celebrate and memorialize the occasion (cf. Luke 9:33). Pentecostal fanfares at Notre Dame University with all their attendant brouhaha are the same kind of misplaced zeal and excessive enthusiasm as building tents on Mount Tabor.

A couple of years ago I was invited to share the leadership of a spiritual life workshop for a very impressive group of robust, well educated, professional religious men. It was a good experience for me except for the day that the Pentecostal leader took over. The nauseating quality of that day reached its peak when all of us—hefty, feisty specimens of mankind, vehement followers of Christ, teachers and rulers of men—found ourselves sitting in a circle (circles of men have become as popular and downright cute as sewing circles!). We sat in a silence that was as dead, dry, and empty as you'd find in any loony bin. Soon enough, however, the silence was broken by idiotic murmurings, husky hums, spooky sighs, and a sweet, soft hymn. Then came some prayers pronounced in the sickening suppliant tones of effeminacy. All of these prayers that were supposed to be gushing forth from the deep caverns of the Spirit were prissy, precious, and studied.

Then I was seized. I don't know if it was the Spirit in me or my daemon. Even if the latter, I am still grateful, because my prayer brought this boring and degrading session to an abrupt end. I prayed: "My Lord, God, may your wild, glorious and awful Spirit break through all our preposterous pietisms and inelegant egotisms and inspire us to serve you manfully. Amen."

I then went outside and walked for a long time—long enough for the wildness of the desert to restore some dignity and revive my drooping spirit. A question, both funny and frightful, occurred to me: What would I have done if the regal, majestic, unmasked, unspoiled Christ had entered that room and stood in that circle? I knew, without a second thought or a single doubt; I would have died of shame. It was then I decided to do something about the paltriness of Pentecostalism. It is this very paltriness which must be deplored—not Pentecostalism itself nor any individual Pentecostal person.

The Need for Wildness

The constant in these forms of pretty poison is paltriness, the bane of our age, the opposite of passion, the deadly enemy of the great love of God. What we desperately need is wildness. We are over-developed, over-civilized, over-protected, over-crowded, and over-ruled. The youth rebellion is long overdue. The recent stampede of city folks to the wild places of America is bound to increase. We all know about Henry David Thoreau and why he went to the woods:

> I went to the woods because I wished to live deliberately, to front only the essential facts of life, and see if I could not learn what it had to teach, and not, when I came to die, discover that I had not lived. [8]

Thoreau knew that no man could live well without some wildness. "I would not have every part of a man cultivated," he insisted. To try to subject everything in man to rational and conscious control would .be to warp, diminish, and barbarize him. So too, the reduction of all nature to profitable use would result in the dehumanization of man. The ruthlessness and savagery that the Puritan had projected onto nature turned out to be within himself. When man turned the green forests into asphalt jungles what he bought was a jungle life. The savagery of urban man, un-

---

8. Henry David Thoreau, *Walden: on the Duty of Civil Disobedience* (New York: Holt, Rinehart and Winston, 1948), p. 74.

tempered by wilderness discipline, was savagery for its own sake.

C. S. Lewis claims that the ubiquitous presence of dogs in civilized places is due to their ability to link man with the wilds. A good beginning, no doubt, but nowhere near enough. We need far wilder things and more wilderness places to ready us for the absolutely unmitigated wildness of God.

A few years ago Mr. Carl D'Aquila, President of the Mesabi Tire Company in Hibbing, Minnesota, invited me to conduct a retreat for a group of men and women in a lodge in northern Minnesota. One evening I went for a long walk. A huge hulk of a bear came lumbering out of the woods, caught up with me on the lonely road and walked with me for a mile or so until a garbage can came between us. That was a brush with wildlife and a feeling for God I really needed.

Yesterday a porcupine waddled away from me and up a nearby tree. Half way up he stopped and scrutinized me, decided I was no threat and came back down, walked over to where I stood, brushed ever so lightly against me and wandered a short distance away to eat some ferns. I felt privileged by such a precarious proximity to wildlife.

In our relationship with God, precarious closeness is a crucial dimension. In fact, what assures the supernatural character of a mystical experience is the persistent polarity in the relationship: the threatening advent of God, and the inevitable and proper tendency on the part of man to withdraw in awe.

Animals can reveal more than the wildness of God. Gentleness, tenderness, and fidelity are hardly ever more impressive than in the animal world. Animals can come close to revealing the very essence of God.

We watched one of our Salukis (the oldest breed of dog in the world) reenact the whole sacrificial love mystery of Christ. Yin was a dog so gentle and loving he hurt nothing. He moved with such exquisite grace and astonishing speed he could catch coyotes; but he just played with them and let them go. One day a neighbor who could not resist a running target, shot him and left a huge hole in his chest. The Saluki managed to return home, leaving a telltale trail of blood behind him, and suffered enormously for two days while we tried in vain to save him. The way this innocent, beautiful God-glorifying creature was so ruthlessly murdered by the blind brutality of a selfish man not only reminded us of the passion of Christ but actually embodied it. This redemptive aspect of the tragedy softened our anger just enough to let the neighbor live.

I am sure that it is the wildest aspects of animal life that glorify God so much; they soften his anger, and he lets us live. Evelyn Underhill has something to say about this to C. S. Lewis:

> . . . Where, however, I do find it impossible to follow you, is in your chapter on animals. "The tame animal is in the deepest sense the only natural animal . . . the beasts are to be understood only in their relation to man and through man to God." This seems to me frankly an intolerable doctrine and a frightful exaggeration of what is involved in the primacy of man. Is the cow which we have turned into a milk machine or the hen we have turned into an egg machine really nearer the mind of God than its wild ancestor? This seems like saying that the black slave is the only natural negro. You surely *can't* mean that, or think that the robin redbreast in a cage doesn't put heaven in a rage but is regarded as an excellent arrangement. Your own example of the good-man, good-wife, and good-dog in the homestead is a bit smug and utilitarian, don't you think, over against the wild beauty of God's creative action in the jungle and deep sea? And if we ever get a sideway glimpse of the animal-in-itself, the animal existing for God's glory and pleasure and lit by His light (and what a lovely experience that is!), we don't owe it to the Pekinese, the Persian cat or the canary, but to some wild free creature living in completeness of adjustment to Nature a life that is utterly independent of man. And this, thank Heaven, is the situation of all but the handful of creatures we have enslaved. Of course I agree that animals too are involved in the Fall and await redemption and transfiguration. (Do you remember Luther looking up from Romans 8:21 and saying to his dog, "Thou too shalt have a golden tail"?) And man is no doubt offered the chance of being the mediator of that redemption. But not by taming, surely? Rather by loving and reverencing the creatures enough to leave them free. When my cat goes off on her own occasions I'm sure she goes with God—but I do not feel so sure of her theological position when she is sitting on the best

chair before the drawing-room fire. Perhaps what it all comes to is this, that I feel your concept of God would be improved by just a touch of wildness . . .[9]

It is true of us all. Our idea of God, our style of life, our capacity for love would all be vastly improved and impassioned by a touch of wildness. No wonder wildness dominates biblical revelation and characterizes the God-man relationship! It is time then to attend more specifically to this central biblical theme: the desert experience. The desert experience is a potent antidote for our pretty poisons, an excoriation of our paltriness, a flaming violent death blow to every vestige of waste that "remains and kills." And the Judaic-Christian desert is peopled with some of the wildest and most passionate heroes in history.

---

9. *The Letters of Evelyn Underhill,* ed. Charles Williams (London: Longmans, Green, 1943), p. 302.

5: The Desert Experience

"The desert experience" is an expression coined over fourteen years ago to characterize the eremitical life at Nada Ranch, the Spiritual Life Institute's first contemplative center in Sedona, Arizona. The outstanding features of this life are simplicity, silence, and solitude. This humanized situation seems to be the most appropriate setting to experience the passion of God breaking through in our lives. The Nada desert is a contemporary American version of the dominant theme of the Bible, the central experience of Israel and the whole Church.

We don't have to romanticize or socialize the desert. The God of Israel was not a reflection of the desert, he was also present in the cities. But in the cities of the Old Testament, man was so driven by lust for power, pleasure, money and honor that he never sought God there. It was man who needed the utter simplicity, the silence and solitude, the emptiness of the desert. In the desert the difference between essentials and nonessentials is reasserted; the distinction between the vital and the moribund is rediscovered. The desert is a destruction of mediocrity which is compromise worked out into a system. Mediocrity becomes impossible in the desert where everything is reduced to the rigid alternatives of life and death. Man then rises up out of a sluggish culture, regains a classical human stature as he responds to reality with authenticity and sensitivity according to a hierarchy of values in accord with the Supreme Value of ultimate reality. And so, in the Judaic-Christian tradition the desert is not merely a natural phenomenon. It is a way of life.

Without the desert experience, man cannot achieve his destiny or fulfill his vocation. It does not matter whether or not he experiences the physical desert. Nor does it matter whether the desert experience takes an ancient or modern form. But it cannot take any random form. This point needs to be stressed. The desert experience is a particular and distinctive experience whose purity must be preserved. This is no easy task once the expression catches the fancy of a fairly large number of people. A popularization of this phrase is just beginning and a distortion of its biblical meaning is noticeable. People, for instance, are using the "desert experience" to designate and even justify a dehumanized and derivative existence in the city, an inexcusable enslavement to a family, an addiction to work, a willingness to live without beauty and leisure, a political-cultural decline. I hope that this brief reflection on the true desert experience and its inherent qualities will dispel the false notions apparent in these absurd examples.

The Essence of the Desert

A striking feature of the desert experience is the physicality of the wilderness. Biblical references to the wilderness and the monumental events that occurred there are not in every instance references to the physical desert, but always to similar places that share certain geographical characteristics: mountaintops, seasides, lakesides, hill countries, and woods. They are always uncrowded, naturally beautiful, uncluttered, unhurried, solitary and still; where one might become reborn, free to be one's best self.

From Jerusalem's towers or its neighboring hills you see lots of desert. And it is to this day a howling desert of waste. Ask Bishop James Pike's widow. People still perish in the deserts of the United States as well as Syria and Arabia. You will not survive in the desert unless you affirm wholeheartedly and quickwittedly its reality and come to terms with its brute surd facts.

The desert is a challenge, an invitation to a contest: whether or not man can come to terms with the bare and undiminished facts of reality—the reality of his deluded and denatured self, his devastated and dehumanized world, and the reality of God. You are not expected to master the elements of the desert, but if you will cope with them you had better master yourself. The candor and honesty of the desert tend inexorably to break through your masks, illusions, and deceits.

Man needs to stand in the desert under the noonday sun and see things as they really are: not managed, dominated, packaged; but wild, dead, uncontrollable. Man needs this confrontation with the wild, untamed forces of nature. He has trifled too long in the genteel tradition. He has not dug deeply enough. He has slipped too easily into a spinsterish concern for the pretty instead of the beautiful, for happiness instead of fullness and truth. He has come to think of the natural world as a condition instead of a great force, and he is content to experience it only superficially—a far cry from Maurice Blondel's description of life as the "experience of the inexhaustible."

In *Walden*, Henry David Thoreau says:

> We can never have enough of nature. We must be re-freshed by the seacoast with its wrecks, the sight of inexhaust-ible vigor, vast and titanic features, the wilderness with its liv-ing and decayed trees, the thundercloud, and the rain which lasts three weeks and produces freshets. We need to witness our own limits transgressed, and some life pasturing freely where we never wander . . . I love to see that nature is so rife with life that myriads can be afforded to be sacrificed and suf-fered to prey on one another; that tender organizations can be so serenely squashed out of existence like pulp—tadpoles which herons gobble up, tortoises and toads run over in the road; and that sometimes it has rained flesh and blood! . . . Poison is not poisonous after all, nor are our wounds fatal.[1]

Powerful as our weapons are, vast as is the destruction of which we are capable, there is something still more powerful than we are. That something is in part the least amicable but also the oldest and most enduring aspect of what Thoreau called "wilder-ness," and it may survive when we have destroyed the better order we tried to make. By managing nature we may to some ex-tent discipline it. We may also, in the process of becoming human, shift somewhat the emphases in its complex of impulses and powers. But we cannot dispense with the wilderness without becoming near-machines and therefore less, not more, than the animal we try to transcend. And so our man-centered humanism backfires and dehumanizes us.

The desert is a place where an egotistic and complacent humanism will not do. It will undo us. Each man must come to

---

1. Thoreau, *op. cit.* p. 265.

terms actively with the evil forces within himself. The Word of God calls us to take the initiative against our own evil; we must accept that responsibility. For original sin is not just an isolated difficulty or an occasional failure. Original sin means that our whole life was once organized for disaster, for destruction, for death.

The Israelites' first sin was their desire to gratify their evil inclinations. This was also the basic temptation of the Corinthians. Paul did not seem to be as much concerned about any particular form of sin or disorder as he was about the essence of sin, man's sinful nature, life determined by the flesh (Gal. 5:17). That is our basic sin: a general, pervasive disorientation, rather than a specific act. Our central human thrust is subtly but decisively misdirected. Our whole life is based on the principles and alternatives of the old world to which Christ, the new man, has already and definitely laid the axe. To persist in this steady, stubborn effort to stuff God into the religious projections of this unreal but factual and intricate world of the flesh is to compund the complexities and absurdities of the world. The cure, ceremoniously, is baptism; existentially, the desert experience. In response to the Spirit we must take the initiative in reforming, in reconstructing our life in Christ. This is what God has in mind for us when he calls us into the desert.

The desert evokes a man's latent capacity for initiative, exploration, evaluation. It interrupts his ordinary pattern of life. It intercepts the stultifying process of a conventional routine piety. It disengages him from a regular round of respectable human activities. Man learns to be still, alert, perceptive, recollected so that issues become clear, reality becomes recognizable and unambiguous. He sees real things, not mere shadows; experiences events, not merely a succession of pseudo-events; knows himself, not merely a projected or statistically polled image of himself. He knows God, not abstractions about God, not even the theology of God, but the much more mysterious God of theology—the God of Abraham, of Moses, of Elijah, of Peter, Paul, and John, of the Fathers of the desert—the God of saints and the God of sinners.

Desert spirituality means much more than getting out of the "rat race." Even the human Christ needed periods of solitary prayer, times set apart. Deep down in every man is the ineluctable need to recognize and proclaim God's absolute sovereignty. We have a need, however hidden, to turn completely to God, a need for a kind of suspension of our horizontal relation with other creatures. And if we manage to go through life without this need ever rising above the threshold of consciousness, it simply proves how gutted and distorted our humanity is, how completely disordered our sense of values!

Even as natural men we are not fully alive until we respond to the periodic need to turn from our passing human activities, to stand before God and belong exclusively to him. What then should be our experienced need as a child of God is to turn habitually with loving trust to the Father and forget everything but him and his care for us. This, too, is the prudence of the desert, wisdom in action.

But even this witness to the claim that God and the things of God have upon us is not the deepest meaning of the desert tradition of spirituality. The desert is, above all, the place where we encounter God, the place where God visits his people. This is why the tradition of desert spirituality has persisted in the Church.

The complexity of civilization vanishes in the desert. Life is reduced to a very few simple decisions, and a wrong decision may be fatal. Living, really living, is a full-time job. There is no other way to survive. The desert is no place for diversions, distractions, luxuries, or trivia.

The only way to God is the way of the real. The desert shatters our managerial complacency, our arrogant lethargy, our spiritual torpor, our barren, bloodless dalliance with the pretty poison of life, and forces us into conjunction with the real, with history. This stark reality does not evoke aggressiveness or romanticism, but pure, unadulterated humanness.

John McKenzie, my chief authority for the biblical desert experience,[2] is so impressed by the ravenous reality of the desert that he calls it evil. I would rather think of it and treat it as an untamed and wild, sometimes ferocious form of good. Even in the tamer desert of Northern Arizona, the Spiritual Life Institute has been whipped and walloped by the ferocity of the desert. We have

---

2 John McKenzie, *Vital Concepts of the Bible* (Wilkes-Barre, Pa.: Dimension Books, 1967).

been washed out and marooned by flash floods, scorched by the merciless brilliance of the sun, and snowed in for weeks by an unusual spectacular blizzard; lightning has struck and fired our trees; torrential rain has eroded our land and seeped through our brand-new buildings; wind has torn off our roofs; our animals have been killed by larger and wilder animals as well as by savage and barbarous neighbors; and we ourselves have been threatened by Sedona citizens, who, ironically, are not wilder than we are but who are so tamed and so retired that newness, freshness, divine wildness—the scandal of Christ—fill them with such repulsion and fear that they resort, typically, to violence. So many of them come to the desert not for the biblical desert experience but for isolated splendor and private pleasure. Psalm 28 is probably as meaningful to us at Nada Ranch as it was to the Jews in Palestine: "The voice of the Lord shakes the wilderness; the Lord shakes the wilderness of Kadesh."

The central, pervading atmosphere of the desert is death. That is why it plays such a vastly important role in the Jewish and Christian traditions and in the monasticism of both the East and the West. But it is not all that glum and bleak. The beauty of the desert is spectacular! The life you find there in tenacious trees, blooming cactuses, and wild flowers is as startling as the death you find in dry creek beds, sunbleached bones, and blowing "dust-devils."

The desert experience is not all darkness and dread but light and joy in the Lord who is sheer delight. The manifestation of God's glory is an indispensable element in the desert experience of both Old and New Testament. Yahweh didn't call his people out of Egypt and into the desert for nothing, *nada*, but for nothing but God, the all, to live fully and exuberantly in the divine milieu of th Promised Land. This is the recurrent biblical theme of the passover, the *Pascha Christi*, reaching its climax with blazing clarity in the Gospels.

The divine summons to man is always a call into wilderness, a vocation to recover the life of paradise after suffering temptation with Christ in desert solitude. In fact, the Transfiguration, which was part of Jesus's desert experience, was the Father's confirmation of Christ's commitment and fidelity to his desert vocation. His perseverance led him finally to death, Mount Calvary the culmination of the desert vocation, and the Resurrection the final, dramatic vindication of his desert life and his sacrificial death. Until then, his disciples persisted in their blindness precisely because they refused to surrender totally to their own desert vocation. In other words, the disciples were unable to see and accept all the implications of Christ's teaching in their own lives because of their unwillingness to suffer. After the Resurrection, of course, particularly after Pentecost, they were transformed. They ceased to be fussbudgets, wasting time and energy caring for themselves. They were kept alive by God's love and nourished by his word and his bread.

Christ's disciples embraced the real desert, which is a long, arduous trek through purgation into Paradise. This experience begins with the free, deliberate decision to suffer; it ends with the uproariously happy surprise of being in harmony with the universe, in the glory of God's presence and incalculably in love with all that is.

The Old Testament Desert

The first and classic encounter of God and man in the desert occurs in the vision of Moses. No one but God could have compelled Moses to do what he did. "If you please, Lord, send someone else," he pleaded. "I have never been eloquent, neither in the past, nor recently, nor now that you have spoken to your servant; but I am slow of speech and tongue" (Ex. 4:14, 10). "Who am I that I should go to Pharaoh and lead the Israelites out of Egypt?" (Ex. 3:11). Moses led Israel out of the pleasurable captivity of Egypt with her "cucumbers, melons, leeks, onions and garlic" (Num. 11:6) into the relentlessly harsh desert to find God in whose name Moses spoke. In the blazing empty expanses of Sinai, Israel could not hide from Yahweh as she could in the fields of Egypt and the cities of Canaan. Israel had to be exposed to God's holy scrutiny, and, in the teeth of death, to discover her destiny and rise again to God's awful summons. God's imperious call required of Israel a passionate response without reservation or bargaining of any kind. Yahweh is a desert God: Israel must deal with him on his own terms—or else. The covenant which

sustained Israel and evoked the marvels of God was formed in the
desert. And that's where God revealed his name and gave his law.
The three central spectacular events in the history of Israel occurred in the desert.

Obedience to a divine call brings into the dreadful wilderness
of Sinai those God chose to fashion into his own people. He leads
them. through the open gates of death into the paradise of the
Promised Land. He strips them of all securities and superfluities,
but by revealing his Name he thus places them directly in communication with his own divine power as a source of unfailing help.
The whole covenant hinges on this intimate act of personal and
profound trust.

When the Israelites failed to trust Yahweh in the wilderness
they were not simply weak, limp, and dilatory; they were substituting the Golden Calf for the ineffable Name, seeking to shorten
the time of suffering by resorting to human expedience dressed up
with religious veneer. Nothing but the divine initiative could restore the violated covenant by reawakening in the people a true
sense of their desert vocation. They had to grasp once again the
meaning of their desert calling: a complete and continual dependence on God alone; and they had to face up to their terrible
propensity toward betrayal and infidelity.

The desert has always been a place of testing. Anyone who
reads the divine office is familiar with this idea in Psalm 94:
"Harden not your hearts, as at Meriba, as on the day at Massah
in the wilderness, when your fathers tested me, and put me to the
proof, though they had seen my work."

In the desert, Israel put Yahweh himself to the test, and this
is peculiar to her tradition. Yahweh was tested; his love and fidelity were proven everlasting and unwavering. Essentially, however, the desert is God's testing ground for man. Israel survived her
desert experience by outfighting and outwitting the elements and
the emptiness, by abandoning herself to God who carried her in
his arms as a father carries his child.

Elijah was the next great desert man in biblical history.
Israel had regressed and taken on all the baggage and bondage of
the overcivilized Canaanite cities. So Elijah walked forty days and
nights into the desert to find Yahweh where he had first revealed
himself to Israel. There in eremitical solitude, Elijah became a

God-intoxicated man and a prominent, crucial figure in the most pressing and dramatic issues of his day.

Elijah resolved the problems of the Jews with desert directness. Fearlessly facing the full assembly of his countrymen on Mount Carmel, he lashed out at their indecision with the stringent words: "How long, O Israel, do you limp between two sides? If the Lord be God, follow him! But if Baal, then follow him" (1 K. 18:21). He then challenged the priests of Baal to a showdown of strength, a trial by fire. Elijah was unyielding, unstinting. He learned the desert lesson of reality and clung to it tenaciously. On this bedrock, steadfastly, he took his bold stand: "The Lord lives—before whose face I stand" (1 K. 17:1). These words comprise the shortest and most effective autobiography ever written. Their effect was immediate and brought down from heaven a lightning bolt of flame upon the altar, giving Israel a sure sign of the right side to be on. These words have remained the charter of all contemplatives ever since, particularly Carmelites, who regard Elijah as their spiritual father.

Elijah not only settled political, social, and moral crises, but even a weather crisis of three years' drought. The narrative in 1 Kings indicates that he was a man on the move, propelled here and there by the Spirit's "Get thee hence!" He did not escape into the desert; he refueled there.

Such a picture may conflict with our preconceived ideas of the contemplative's role, despite the fact that Thomas Merton spoke and wrote more knowledgeably about our present social predicament than anyone else I know. We are too prone to picture a contemplative as a niminy-piminy pious chap unable to survive the hurly-burly of the world. Elijah, the "hairy" desert man, loins girt with leather belt, was one of those rare men who seem to be absolutely fearless; he excoriated kings and their henchmen. He was a wild unstemmable colossus of God. He was Yahweh's great working model of a broad and healthy contemplation integrated into the whole of human life. He stood stout and stalwart like a signpost on the human highway, a signpost that read: "God ahead!" Thank God for modern hermits as charmingly sturdy and wholesomely radical and socially alert as Thomas Merton and ancient hermits as wild and wooly and worldly as Elijah!

The whole world suffers enormously today from a paucity of leadership. Every single head of state is being carried along by events and no longer "with honor." The Church scene is no brighter. We need a desert man of the stature of Elijah who will fulminate effectively against "limping between two sides," and illuminate the way out of our morass by grassroots contemplation.

Almost a hundred years later, another prophet arose. Hosea lamented Israel's tragic infidelity and, recognizing only one possibility for her spiritual regeneration, urged Israel to return to the desert. "God will espouse you, lead you into the desert, and there speak to your heart" (Hos. 2:14). If Israel returned to the simple, harsh reality of the desert, deprived of the wealth and luxuries of Canaan, Hosea believed she would recognize once again the spouse of her youth. I don't know of any more cogent and succinct summation of the spiritual life than Hosea's pungent acclamation.

There you have biblical religion, the spirituality of the West, in a nutshell: God in search of man, taking the initiative, making the overtures. Then he leads man into the desert—away from small passions, frivolous pleasures and vapid peace; out of the mazes of the mind, beyond symbols and words; so that man might discover the Signified, the Word unspoken, in the darkness that veils the source of his being. Then and there in desert emptiness, as in the virginal emptiness of Mary, God speaks to the heart.

The New Testament Desert

Recalling the desert origins of Israel's faith, John the Baptist announced the biggest crisis in the history of Israel. Unless the Jews left their homes and business and went out into the desert to hear his announcement, they would not likely hear it at all.

The "voice crying in the wilderness" (Mt. 3:3) found the Jews not merely inquisitive, checking out a solitary ascetic living alone in the desert until the day came for him to speak. They were receptive and responsive, a people ruled by a supereminent thirst for God, driven to the water, to the fountain of living waters that can keep a nation alive forever.

This desert man in animal skins, feeding on locusts and wild honey, seemed to know where the living fountain was. So the people followed him into the desert and listened. When John spoke, his words were powerful. Like Samuel, they did not "fall to the ground" (1 Sam. 3:19-20); like Jeremiah, they were put into his mouth live, by God, "to destroy and to overthrow, to build and to plant" (Jer. 1:10); like Isaiah, his lips were purged with a burning coal from the altar of God (Is. 6:6-7); and like Ezekiel, he must speak whether others listened or not (Ezech. 2:5-6).

John was a man of action and called for action. He lived totally in the present and refused to delay. He was a man of one consuming passion and skipped all second-rate pleasures. He had a singular mission and would not be sidetracked.

John was not the Messiah. He said plainly he was not the Christ. He was a voice, an announcer, another signpost, pointing away from himself to someone who was to come after him. He described himself as the best man awaiting the bridegroom, the servant awaiting his master, "the lachet of whose sandal I am not worthy to unloose" (Mt. 3:11). John was the immediate precursor of Jesus, and his whole purpose was to prepare for Christ.

Jesus is *the* desert man. He was not essentially, as so many modern theologians erroneously believe, the man for others. Altruistic unto his death on the cross, utterly selfless and totally expended for all, he was still essentially something else: the man *from* the Other, the Wholly Other. That is why he was a silent solitary; that is why he was always going out to the desert and into the sea and onto the mountaintops—because of the supreme reality of his Father. And it was his Father's absorbing, compelling presence that empowered him to be, consequently, the man for others.

In St. Mark's "desert gospel," Jesus is a wilderness man. The crucial events in his life occur in wilderness places. Yet for Mark the wilderness is not primarily locality but a theme full of theological implications.

What happened to Jesus in the desert during those forty days was not limited to that period and that place. Throughout his entire ministry the Spirit continued to drive him to the wilderness, only beginning with the baptism of John.

Jesus submitted himself to John's baptism, manifesting his own willingness to endure God's judgment and even to die for the sins of the people. After his baptism he was led by the Spirit into the desert to be tempted, to live under the judgment of God. This is a highly significant sequence of events in the life of Christ, and should be pondered on by Pentecostal groups that burlesque the baptism of the Spirit. Jesus's desert experience was the necessary outcome of his baptism, unfeigned and unconditional. His return to the desert was no strategic move in view of a future coup. It was no temporary retreat in preparation for an active mission. Mark does not consider Jesus's miracles, healings and debates as final triumphs. In them the struggle takes shape, but is not ultimately won. When Christ withdrew into solitude he was not retreating but renewing his attack on the power of evil. It was in the wilderness that the *decisive* cosmic struggle took place. It always does.

The wilderness reminds us of a deeper level of history undergirding the tangible events of Christ's ministry. The desert marked him indelibly as God's man and Satan's enemy. To live in this state of struggle with the Adversary of God, and to persevere in this conflict in direct and complete dependence on God himself, eschewing the political, economic, and spiritual powers of the three temptations, and remaining utterly poor—this is the wilderness life. Such a life may unfold far from the physical desert. But if Christ needed to withdraw periodically into silence and solitude, it seems egregious presumption to assume that we can go on forever on our own steam with no direct and intimate contact with the infinite Source of our being. Despite the suspicions of "secular Christianity," withdrawal to a desert solitude is not only justifiable but praiseworthy.

After St. Paul's dramatic conversion on the road to Damascus, he immediately went straight to the Arabian desert and spent a long time there. Obviously, the full meaning of his vocation could not be penetrated unless he returned to the traditional source of spiritual strength, the place where man meets God. Only after he had steeled himself by a prolonged retreat in the desert did Paul plunge into his exhausting apostolic endeavors in the crowded bustling cities.

The desert tradition continued among the Desert Fathers who abandoned the cities of the pagan world to live in solitude. By the fourth century the deserts of Egypt, Palestine, Arabia, and Persia were teeming with hermits in quest of salvation which today we would term authenticity, integrity or wholeness. The

Desert Fathers refused to drift along in a questionable society. But they were not escapists. They met the problems of their time; in fact, they were way ahead of their times, and opened the way for a new man and a new society, shaping the whole history of the Church and the Western world. They were axial or marginal men. They were like live fish, the vital, valiant kind you see jumping out of their natural, comfortable habitat, leaping into man's domain, drinking in his oxygen. Such saltatory stunts and suprarational stuff kill any ordinary run-of-the-mill fish. The Fathers were not passive pawns of a decadent state nor soft, mollycoddle members of a conventional society. Their flight was positive and dynamic, not negative and fearful.

What the Fathers sought most of all was their own true self, in Christ. They rejected their false self, fabricated under the crazy compulsions and phoney values of the world. They chose an unmapped way to God, a God no one knew except by experience. In the arid desert they were weaned away from their old pictures, images, and ideas of God, and were readied for what the desert was and is always meant to disclose: the unknown God in the cloud of unknowing.

The Fathers went into the desert to pray, to feed on God. What was at the heart of their experience? Death: no attachment to their own egos or their own desires or plans or achievements; no identification with their superficial, transient, narcissistic selves. The Fathers had to die to the values of an ephemeral existence as Christ had died to them on the cross, and rise from the dead with him in the light of an intensely new wisdom. And so the pampered ego was purged away, and the real self and Christ became one Spirit.

The Desert Today

It wasn't long before the physical desert became inaccessible to most people. Yet the desert experience, as we have seen, is central and essential to all the People of God. That is why the Church instituted Lent—so that everyone could experience the desert. A soft diluted Lent will do no good. Lent must be characterized by hardy asceticism: a relentless struggle with daemons, an athletic slimming down for battle, a simplified life, a holy poverty, a clearer vision, a fierce and universal love, a long loving look at the real, an emptiness—all a preparation for the fullness of God.

The retreat, too, is meant to provide the desert experience. How disastrous it would be, then, to turn retreats into dialogues, performances, brain-storming, sensitivity or therapy sessions. These opportunities ought to be provided for those who need them; but nothing ought to take the place of the retreat as the desert experience. And everyone, particularly the religious leader, ought to have prolonged periods when he can really return to the desert.

Monasticism should be an authentic desert experience. Monastic life should not only give a wilderness witness to people in the secular world, but should actually provide quiet wilderness opportunities for all those city dwellers and neurotic activists who are engaged in what Faulkner called a "frenzied steeplechase toward nothing." Unfortunately, most monasteries in this country have become beehives of buzzing activists themselves, and in this incredible foofaraw they have lost their monastic vocation, their desert calling—their only way of feeding the multitudes: by providing a specially sacred time and place to be still.

The original members of my own monastic order, the Carmelites, were hermits, simple laymen, living as solitaries in a loosely connected group, in caves and huts on the side of Mount Carmel. You might call this style of life an informal lay monasticism. Contemplation was the unique purpose of life—not excluding other activities, but dominating them. In other words, the hermits worked in a way appropriate to a life where prayer was primary. They "meditated day and night on the Law of the Lord" unless engaged in "some other just occupation." According to *The Fiery Arrow*, the earliest document originating within the Carmelite Order, by Nicholas the Frenchman, Prior General of the Order, they were vehemently opposed to the prostitution of the eremitical life:

> Conscious of their imperfection, the hermits of Carmel persevered for a long time in the solitude of the desert but as they intended to be of service to their neighbor, in order not to

be guilty of infidelity to their way, they went sometimes, but rarely, down from their hermitage. That which they had harvested with the sickle of contemplation, in solitude, they went to thresh on the threshing floor of preaching, and to sow it abroad on all sides.[3]

The hermits lived wholeheartedly as witnesses of God's transcendence, bearing the awful burden of divine passion.

Centuries later, Carmelite foundations were established in Europe. The Holy See placed them in the ranks of the Mendicant Orders, and like the other Orders, the hermits became overorganized, overcrowded, and overworked. Once they moved out of the desert, they lost their unique and invaluable charism and ceased to make their distinct contribution to the Church and to human culture. In aligning itself with the Mendicants, the Carmelite Order sacrificed its own true and unique identity as an order of apostolic hermits.

In the sixteenth century, St. Teresa and St. John of the Cross were pressed by God to restore the primitive ideal. As part of their reform they resorted to the cloistered accoutrements held in such horror today by so many good people: walls, grills, laws of silence, veils. This was not due to the unhealthy influence of the Turks, a popular opinion generated today by a few critics who seem exceedingly anxious to modernize. The Teresian reform took on these cloistered features to make the eremitical life possible in the distracted urban life of Europe.

A Spanish disciple of St. Teresa, Thomas of Jesus, amplified the movement and solidified it by establishing in the last years of the sixteenth century at Bolarque a distinct Desert House where the Carmelites led a strictly eremitical life. Although the Order has since become less eremitical, Carmel is inconceivable without its Desert Houses. They make realizable the original purpose of Carmel: to offer to God a pure heart. Only disciplined wild men who come into passionate possession of themselves are capable of such a high priestly oblation.

Such is the desert experience! Without it a Carmelite is des-

---

3. Thomas Merton, *Disputed Questions* (New York: Farrar, Straus and Cudahy, 1953), p. 221.

titute and impotent and ought to take very seriously the following rebuke of his father, St. John of the Cross:

> O souls created for these heights! O you who are called to possess them! What are you doing with your time? With what are you busying yourself? Your aims are base and your goods but miseries. . . .[4]

Some of us took St. John seriously, and in 1960 the Spiritual Life Institute of America was founded in the Spirit of Elijah, in the tradition of Carmel. I was joined at first by George Hoyt, a modern God-seeking nomad; Don Thorman, now publisher of *The National Catholic Reporter*; and shortly afterwards, my brother Liam McNamara. We began to explore the possibilities of introducing into our American culture more viable and authentic forms of both monasticism and lay-contemplative life. After a good deal of roadwork, seminaring, and some significant conversations with Thomas Merton, we came to a remarkable conclusion: what seemed to be the most fitting contemporary form of contemplative life turned out to be the most ancient monastic model, the primitive Carmelite form of eremiticism. A desire to be completely and immediately at the disposal of God lies at the root of eremiticism. Among us there is a marked preference for solitary contemplation. Our common life is primarily a matter of common sympathy and common aspiration for the ultimately real, for union with God himself in personal passionate spousal relationship.

Our quest for a contemporary style of contemplative life that would ring with authenticity drove us back into ancient anchoritic forms of monastic life. But Carmel is not the only model. The Dead Sea Scrolls have revealed another, Qumran, an apocalyptic community that imitated the ancient sojourn in the wilderness of Sinai. In fact, the aim of Qumran and our Nada communities in Arizona and Nova Scotia are the same, namely: "the purity of paradise truth recovered within the fellowship of a disciplined

---

4. St. John of the Cross, "Spiritual Canticle" from *The Collected Works of St. John of the Cross*, trans. by Kieran Kavanaugh and Otilio Rodriguez O.C.D. (Garden City, N.Y.: Doubleday and Co. Inc., 1964), p. 559 (retranslation).

wilderness encampment sustained by the Spirit." Eremitical life is the extreme means to the perfection of the contemplative life, and the ideal and norm of monasticism. St. John of the Cross expressed the eremitical goal in these words:

> Now I occupy my soul
> And all my energy in this service;
> I no longer tend the herd,
> Nor have I any other work
> Now that my every act is love. [5]

In 1963 the Spiritual Life Institute took St. John so seriously that we dropped everything and went to the desert. It was not the wildest desert in America by any means, but it was available, so we journeyed to Oak Creek Canyon, very close to the town of Sedona. Oak Creek is one of the most beautiful canyons in the world and Sedona one of the most physically attractive but also one of the most spiritually dead towns in the whole country. A recently published book on the safest places to live in the U.S. included Sedona, another town built, ruled, and governed on the principles of safety rather than the principles of sanctity, even though the latter alone can provide the basic structure for a Christian community.

Sedona lies in the high desert of Northern Arizona. And it was there that the most ancient form of contemplative life in the Western world was reborn and nurtured in the shape of Nada, the first desert house of the Spiritual Life Institute. Nada was not actually named, however, and did not really take shape until Tessa Bielecki arrived in 1967. With her extraordinary combination of Teresian qualities she gave Nada the life that now fills it to the brim and overflows so opulently.

I wasn't in the desert long before I recognized why God raised his people there: the awful scale of the thing, the suggestion of virginity, the fusion of angelic and daemonic elements with the pure earth, untrammelled and untouched by anything humanly contrived.

Government officialdom defines a wilderness as "a minimum

------

5. *Ibid*, p. 413.

of not less than 5,000 contiguous acres of roadless area." But infinitely more than that is involved. The wilderness invokes nostalgia—justified, reasonable, unsentimental—a nostalgia for the lost America and the pilgrim Church, the rugged nation and the robust community of believers our forefathers knew. It means something lost and something still present; it seems remote and forbidding and at the same time intimate; it feels like it has worked its way into our blood and nerves; it is frightening, but still draws us into its tantalizing haunts, its unbearable heat; it tones up our nerves and brings to life again those emotions that have not yet been irreparably stunned, deadened, numbed by the caterwauling of commerce, the sweating scramble for profit and prestige. It stretches beyond us without limit.

Here in North Kemptville, Nova Scotia, our other wilderness, I can rest. The desert is different. To me the desert is stimulating, exciting, exacting. I am not inclined to sleep or even to relax. All my senses are sharpened and heightened for a fuller life, for more engaging action, with no other purpose than the goodness of the action itself, because the action is pure contemplation.

The early mornings, evening, and the nights as bright as day, are my favorite desert times. But noon is the crucial hour. That is when the desert reveals itself nakedly and cruelly.

I remember the first time I stood in the middle of the desert and experienced the utter shock of the real: that out there as far as I could see, all that shimmering earth under the scorching sun, is a different world, older and greater and deeper by far than ours, a world which surrounds and sustains the little world of men as sea and sky surround and sustain a ship. At that moment childhood was recaptured, the world of marvels was rediscovered, nothing could be taken for granted. I realized in a brand new fresh way how just being on earth, able to see and touch and hear in the midst of tangible and mysterious things, is such a strange and daring adventure! As an unknown author said:

> Wilderness is no luxury but a necessity of the human spirit, and as vital to our lives as water and good bread. A civilization which destroys what little remains of the wild, the spare, the original, is cutting itself off from its origins and betraying the principle of civilization itself.

If industrial man continues to multiply his numbers and expand his operations he will succeed in his apparent intention, to seal himself off from the natural and isolate himself within a synthetic prison of his own making. He will make himself an exile from the earth and then will know at last, if he is still capable of feeling anything, the pain and agony of final loss.

We have been warned:

Ours is the age of the bulldozer as much as it is the age of the atomic bomb. For good or ill, we need no longer conform to the contours of the earth. The only wilderness that will be left is what we determine shall remain untouched and that other wilderness in the heart of man that only God can touch.[6]

Preserving both these wildernesses demands our best efforts. It ought to grab the attention and fire the imagination of both our social scientists and our religious leaders; it certainly ought to be the chief occupation of monks.

As Father McKenzie says, paraphrasing nicely the acrimonious invectives of Jeremiah: "If men will not return to the desert to find God, he will make their cities a desert where no sound drowns out his voice."

6. George H. Williams, *Wilderness and Paradise in Christian Thought* (New York: Harper and Brothers, 1962), p. 136.

6: From Romance to Mysticism

Our plight today is not unlike the enslaved condition of the Jews in Egypt prior to their liberating desert experience. We have become inextricably entangled in the life of the flesh. We have developed such sophisticated, respectable forms of enslavement that no matter how suffocating they become for the life of the spirit, no one seems to object. It has become possible, for instance, to enthrone the gospel of progress even though this requires the repudiation of the Gospel of Christ and the destruction of the whole edifice of ethics, law, culture, human relationships, and human behavior constructed by the civilization of the West.

Even though Christ said, so simply and clearly, that his Kingdom was not of this world, no one seems upset by the fact that half the Protestant and Catholic theologians in the world are teaching the opposite and that clergymen find an extension of the Gospels in the materialism of Marx and Engels, lay wreaths on the shrine of Lady Chatterly, are a significant segment of the 16,000,000 readers of *Playboy*, and are more and more prone to preach and accept situational ethics, to allow and arrange situational worship—a state of affairs which is not improved by pop groups, folk singers, or even stripteasers. The shaken condition of institutional Christianity does not alarm those randy men of the cloth because they feel that like the state in Marxist mythology, the structure of the Church must wither away. In the meantime priests and nuns are walking out in shoals to resume the material and sensual preoccupations they had renounced forever, so publicly and so surely.

The life of the flesh is governed not only by the gospel of progress but also by the pursuit of happiness. It is supported by science and technology; it is enriched even by religion, once Christianity has been emptied of its spiritual and transcendent content; and, finally, it is embraced by the state. Statesmen pass it on from one to another like a torch held upside down; from Roosevelt to

Truman and Eisenhower; from Kennedy to Johnson to Nixon, Ford, and Carter. But progress and every pursuit is confined within the limits of the flesh and therefore doomed to extinction.

The life of the flesh, which depends on ever-growing prestige and power, is all-consuming and consequently very wearying. Relief is sought in the "mysticism" of sex, a kind of pleasure and excitement which alone offers an additional illusory sense of transcendental satisfaction, notably lacking in another Cadillac, a trip to the Orient, or a bigger and better suburban home.

Sex is the only "mysticism" the materialistic life of the flesh can possibly offer. In the prosaic, workaday world of the flesh you find inevitably and ubiquitously a vast obsessive outpouring of erotica in every shape and form—in book, film, play, and entertainment, in body, word, and deed—so that there is no escape. Every possible sexual pleasure or perversion is available to everyone: the halt and the lame, young and old. Anyone can see it or do it at any time or anywhere—even "in the road," as the Beatles sang to us some years ago. Imagination is no longer required. Feeling is irrelevant. No impediments either! The pill has taken care of that. Now we can have sterile sex and shattering orgasms without a care in the world. Waning happiness calls for another spurt, that's all. If topless shows grow dull, try bottomless. If one man or woman becomes tiresome, take another. Or take two at a time. Or an orgy. Or jump from the rafters and, like swifts, copulate in mid air! It is the flesh that quickens; the spirit profits nothing. If my body can evoke a bodily quiver from another, or vice versa, I call it love and claim that I am alive. An orgasm a day keeps the doctor away! A slight twist of Descartes' famous axiom captures the mood of our sensate culture: *copulo ergo sum*. I copulate, therefore I am.

Since the life of the spirit is forsaken for the life of the flesh, no *metanoia* is possible. So education must do. It has become the equivalent of conversion and has replaced an indispensable formation in the life of the spirit. Through education we talk ourselves into multiple forms of spiritual impoverishment and solve all our problems: alcoholism, drug-addiction, venereal disease, inflation, political corruption, juvenile delinquency. Education may be the greatest con trick or the most false god of all times. But it's the only solution in a world wholly secularized and devoid of the spirit.

That is why it thrills me and seems a sign of great hope to find a man as secular and sophisticated as Malcolm Muggeridge saying so eloquently from the most public pulpits and worldly podiums what I am merely echoing here in my muted, monkish way. But he is a voice crying in the urban wilderness. The Establishment which had honored and respected Mr. Muggeridge for so long is now unnerved by the Jesus he rediscovered and the Gospel he is taking so seriously. No voice seems able to intercept our gadarene descent into the sea.

Previous civilizations have been overthrown from without by the incursion of barbarian hordes; ours has dreamed up its dissolution in the cold, calculating minds of its intellectual elite who nurture barbarians, American style, to perpetuate the comfortable captivity of middle America, and thus guarantee the disintegration of any real American achievement.

There have been in our age some criticisms and protests, but they have been niggardly and negligible. The yearning and burning that fired up so many young people a few years ago seems to have died down. Here and there one notices a spark, a spiritual movement, but never one that is close enough to the center of our culture.

The Life of the "Flesh"

It is not the body that smothers the spirit but the *flesh*. The "flesh" is the generic term not for bodily life, since the body along with the soul is sanctified by the Holy Spirit, but for mundane life. The "flesh" refers not only to cupidity and licentiousness, but even worldly conformism and actions based on human respect or social preoccupation. In this sense, even a good many of our "religious" acts are of the "flesh," as Michael De La Bedoyere helps us understand:

> Are not the tests we instinctively apply those of edification, reputation with others, the show we put up, respectable morality, external statistics, degrees of piety, rejection of the unusual, suspicion of the man who does not play the game, of the "crank," of whosoever ventures to think for himself? Any tests of religious . . . or spiritual worth are, anyway, invidious and dangerous, and their popularity today is a bad sign. God

alone judges the heart, that is, the real man. These popular
tests are really tests of adherence to social conventions in a
religious setting. In a ruder but spiritually sounder age, when
religion was the highest dimension of life and life was integrated with vocation and status, men on whom sound doctrine was
sternly imposed were left personally much freer to find their
own spiritual levels. In other words, they were left to be themselves spiritually. The judgment of God, not the judgment of
their fellows, was what mattered. Such men felt the judgment
of God to be stern, and also the judgment of the State with
which the Church might be linked. But they were relatively
free from the judgment of their fellows. Today we feel the
judgment of our fellows to be stern, but the judgment of God
negligible, because he is all-merciful. The contrast, one feels,
sets off the difference between a religion that inclines to a realism and a religion that inclines to the bourgeois conventions
whose essence is the vulgar endeavor to become better and ending by becoming rather worse.[1]

The "flesh" is our external self, our false self, our public
conventional self. Collectively it is the dehumanized, disoriented
world; individually, it is the alienated person, alienated precisely
because he is inordinately caught up in the intricate and endless
temporalities of the superficial secular world. Flesh in biblical
language refers to the creature left to himself without the Spirit of
God to sustain him. That is what St. John the Evangelist means
when he says "the flesh is of no avail" (John 6:63).

The "spirit" in Jewish thought and especially in St. Paul, is
not something that belongs to man. It is man's *complete self* in action, in love, united to God in Christ. Only the Spirit of God, by
freeing the soul from subjugation to its desires, can restore the
body and soul to the ultimate glory for which God destines the
whole man.

That is exactly what God did in Christ. He was the free
man, the perfect expression of life as God intended it. He was the
life of the world. But the world of the flesh in pursuit of happiness, according to its own natural lights, rejected him. By mur-

---

1. Michael De La Bedoyere, "The Modern Vice," *The Christian Vision*,
ed. by M. E. Evans, Aguin Press (London, 1956), pp. 201-202.

dering Christ, the fulness of life, the utmost reality, the world condemned itself to an extremely limited form of life and a very meagre experience of the real.

The paltriness of our lives, with the consequent crippling frustration, is due no doubt to our blind servitude to the over-developed, supercomplicated world. Sex, drugs, the pursuit of money, power and pleasure, even a little religion, become the means of suppressing a growing sense of futility instead of the means of breaking through at whatever risk to a new kind of reality. There is no way that any dogma, prestige, or temporary un-consciousness can cover up the terrifying absence of meaning, the moral vacuum, in human life. Neither can fanaticism, cynicism, or indifference.

We take this unreal world more earnestly than we take Christ, and live in damnable flesh-imprisonment. We may live *in* the world of the flesh; indeed, we must. But if we are *of* this world, living by its standards, ruled by its values, then there is no hope. And in all honesty we must confess, unless we are saints, that we have betrayed Christ and have forsaken his Kingdom. His Kingdom is forsaken to the extent that our lives are ruled by worldly prudence and convenience rather than the principles of selfless love outlined in Jesus's Sermon on the Mount. We are stuck in the flesh. In that case all the political, social tidying up, all the scientific, technological progress, all the religiosity in the world won't do any good. We cannot serve God and Mammon. We cannot be men of God and men of the world at the same time.

A subtle but very telling example of this is the movement of nonviolence, of passive resistance in the nineteen-sixties. It was not the Christian way of life, the life of the spirit—prayer, pen-ance, self-denying love—in action. It was not a basis for existence. It was not contemplative enough. It was simply another tactic of the flesh, albeit far more admirable, but still a strategy, a tech-nique. This nonviolent scheme did not challenge the other side to change its way of life: and that is the central component of what Gandhi called *satyagraha* or soul-force—the vital capacity to chal-lenge another to the spiritual realm of Being by the power of your own soul. That is what we mean by Christ-life—the realization of love. Isn't it strange that a Hindu should turn out to be the great-est modern example of the way of Christ, the way of suffering love to the point of death? Gandhi's nonviolence was based not on effectiveness but on faith, involving a renunciation of the fruits of action in simple obedience to God's will, a loving, unifying will which in a world of injustice leads inevitably to the cross. Nonviolence in deed, said Thomas Merton, is nothing more than a living out of a nonviolence of the heart, an inner unity already experienced in prayer.

Passion Is the Breakthrough Virtue

Is there a way out of the thralldom of the flesh? Yes there is: passion. Passion breaks through the tight teguments of the flesh and paves the way for the transformation of our lives by the power of the Spirit.

Passion is not the exclusive quest of an egotistic pleasure, but an intense psychological sum of energy that focuses our sensibility and fuses all our faculties into a unified drive toward a supreme value and to particular values that seem to be connected with that ultimate prize. If we are passionate enough, all of our human potentialities are activated and integrated into a free and lively personality, moving us gracefully from conversion, to completion, into communion: from romance to mysticism.

Passion is not merely one emotion or even the sum of all emotions but rather a psycho-physical thrust of the whole body-person toward the goal of all human striving. The loving awareness of what truly satisfies a human being has a strong emotional quality coloring a wide range of deep and daring human relationships, all of which involve the human adventurer in an unconditional and all-pervasive relationship with God—whom we all must ultimately choose. At the beginning, we choose him necessarily and unconsciously; as we become processively human, we choose him freely and consciously. The culminating phases of that humanizing, liberating process are so final and the passion so totally fulfilling that we can appropriately, as we do in the case of Jesus, refer to this triumph as *the passion*. The passion is the pass-over from eros to agape, from the quest to all the rest, from the symbols and the signs to Love itself and the One signified.

According to St. Augustine, passion is the power that drives men toward God, restless until it rests in God. It may take many romantic forms but it must eventually become the living flame of mystical love or it will flicker out. In other words, if you are not a mystic, driven by a transcendental hunger and thirst for God, you are bound to be a playboy or a playgirl; or if you don't have what it takes for that, a voyeur or a shell of a man, ekeing out a quasi-existence on vicarious venereal pleasures.

Passion requires a compelling imaginative symbol on which to focus its energy, and a way of life that will provide ample opportunity for the spirit to break free from the flesh as it grows in mounting momentum from the animated discoveries of romantic love to the divine disclosures of mystical marriage.

The unconscious Reality toward which passion is striving so relentlessly can only be grasped through a symbol, a symbol which relates more to the needs of the subject than to the nature of the object. The temptation is to become attached to the symbol, whether it be my concept of God, a vocation, a vacation, a political, religious, or social cause, or another human being. The symbol, somehow or other, suggests the completion of myself and awakens in me a range of emotions that start racing through the symbol toward the pleroma, the fulfillment of my being through realization of divine union. When the other person ceases to be merely a symbol and becomes a real person, enjoying an existence outside of his function as symbol, that is the beginning of love.

Christ is the most perfect symbol of all. His life and message were both remarkably and incomparably passionate, expressing divine invisibilities and human potentialities. If Christ is our symbol, our passion must harmonize with the Gospel demand for *total* dedication.

Christ's "follow me" is ruthless, ignoring convention and disregarding common decencies and the obligations of normal living. "Let the dead bury the dead" (Mt. 8:22), he told the man who wanted to postpone the proclamation of the Kingdom of God because of family duties. "No one who puts his hand to the plow and looks back is fit for the Kingdom of God" (Lk. 9:62). One must, admittedly, live within the reality of the flesh and manage harmoniously. But when the Spirit makes its demands there is nothing to do but comply. The primacy of the Spirit is expressed in Christ's own formula of authority: "It was said to the men of old . . . but I say to you . . ." (Mt. 5:21-22).

Real passion can be distinguished from its synthetic substitutes. While mere sentiment cares only about the feeling produced, passion is other-directed, spent upon its object. There is also an observable external difference. Genuine passion alters people's behavior and endures beyond physical union with or need for the beloved, even during the course of a long love affair. Since true passion is part of the search for the authentic self, a highly sexual man or woman can remain marvellously indifferent to persons more richly endowed in every way than his or her own spouse.

Even though Blaise Pascal, one of the illustrious intellectuals in history, came under the influence of Jansenism, he was man enough and Christian enough to see and to say that there is no true human greatness without passion. Passion breaks down the static equanimity which some questionable spiritual techniques strive for, and breaks through the exceedingly narrow framework in which reason imprisons us. Hiroshima illustrates what happens when the power of the intellect is cut loose from morality and love. It is obvious that our sick world today has lost its soul. There is hardly a breath of spirit to quicken the spate of ideologies that have sprung up in the last two centuries; and that is why their existence is so transient.

Intellect by itself cannot create the psychic unity of the individual and the social unity of peoples. Only when a single passion takes hold of us, gathering into its wake all dispersed and contradictory efforts, can we achieve personal unity.

St. Thomas Aquinas insisted that to act with passion was more human and therefore more perfect than to act out of merely rational motivation. To act passionately is to act more humanly, and so it is a supra-rational, not a subrational act. Our actions are human to the degree that they are intentional acts of the whole man. You cannot feel your way into the whole truth. Neither can you intellectually conceive the mystery of life. Passion must be enlightened by reason and reason must be kindled by passion.

Integrating the Daemonic

The passionate elements in us—sex, eros, anger, rage, buffoonery, the thirst for knowledge or power, a yearning for solitude or community—are natural: they stimulate our lives and can be constructive or destructive.

In order to be helpful they need to be recognized, affirmed and integrated into the harmonious wholeness of the personality. Sex, for example, should serve the purposes of personal intimacy, whether celibate or married; eros should be ordered in the service of love; anger and rage should be vented through righteous moral indignation; clowning should never succumb to ridicule but remain corybantic relief or a form of apostolic love or education.

These forces in us are called daemonic because they have the power to take over completely. When one of these elemental forces goes awry and controls the entire personality we have "daemon possession" or psychosis.

The opposite of the daemonic is not rational security or peaceful tranquility but a return to the inanimate—passionlessness. Apathy and delayed explosion are the toll exacted by the repression of the daemonic dimensions of being. One instance of such an explosive reaction to the repression of the natural daemonic forces in us is that fetid and murky syllabub: William Blatty's *Exorcist*. The devil-possession that Blatty portrays in Friedkin's film is not the kind we have to worry about. If Satan is going to attack the Kingdom of God every once in a long while by turning a lovely little girl into an ogre, then we can sit back and relax. The worrisome and dangerous figure in Blatty's story is the girl's mother. She was truly possessed; she's the one we must really beware of. The most reliable sources of knowledge of the devil have always claimed that subtlety is his outstanding characteristic. There is no subtlely in *The Exorcist*. It is a bloody, fatal struggle between the devil and his exorcists.

Yet it was a successful book and a big money-making movie. Yes, because our lives are so boringly proper we love squalor; because nothing ever happens to us we enjoy goose pimples; and because we are so depressed by the insignificance and monotony of our lives any facile uplift will do. *The Exorcist* offered all these qualities in one noxious package, plus a combination of prurience and insipid piety that always draws an audience.

A passionless society represses whatever is brutish and hideous. Deplorable explosions such as Blatty's or Friedkin's are bound to occur.

What is manfully required of each of us is a personal, whole-some incorporation of the daemonic into the service of his major project of existence. Without the daemonic aspect our spiritual lives remain vapid and fribbling. And if our daemons are not allowed to make a constructive contribution to the humanization and deification of ourselves then they will play a destructive role.

Repression has prevailed in our century and we have wit-nessed the atrocities committed by man on man in mass murders, unspeakable tortures, and senseless wars. Each one of us harbors in his heart the same savage impulses that led to such outlandish crimes. Unheeded, undirected daemons are bound to assert them-selves furtively; if not in the heinous crimes of Nazism, then in the respectable corruption of the Nixon administration. Repressed daemons drive us to perverted forms of aggression. "Violence is the daemonic gone awry. It is daemon possession in its starkest form,"[2] says Rollo May.

We evade the daemonic to our detriment by losing ourselves in the herd, in the array of men who kill for the nation or for freedom, or in the millions of television watchers who observe vio-lence for entertainment. Thus the daemonic is dispensed by im-personality. The anonymous single man secluded in a New York City room turns out to be the typical killer. He is not alone. He sees, smiles, knows all the television personalities, but he himself is never known. His smile is unseen, his idiosyncrasies unnoticed. This is the horrible tragedy: he remains an unnamed alien isolat-ed in the crowd. As Scripture tells us, to be unnamed was the most severe punishment Yahweh could inflict on his people. "Their names shall be wiped out of the books of the living" (Ex. 32:32; Ps. 69:28; Rev. 3:5).

How did the Jews preserve their name and become a fitting vehicle for the revelation of God's passion? How did the Greeks achieve their superb civilization? They made love, killed, and bled with zest. Their strong men cried. Their wise men chose their passions. They were not driven by them. The daemonic will get the upper hand as long as we continue to run from it. The fer-vent inclusion of these hidden powers, these *evil urges*, into the

---

2. Rollo May, *Love and Will* (New York: Dell Publishing Co., 1969), p. 130.

personal presence of a gracious human being is required for wholeness, and therefore for holiness. Only if these untamed sources of energy are at the service of man, and are consciously and easily—that is, virtuously—available, can human beings live passionately and serve God vigorously.

Passion out of control—lust, for instance—is undoubtedly one of the most destructive forces in the world; but the evil let loose in human life by uncontrolled passion is nothing compared to the passion of love accomplished in the Redemption, and accessible to all the followers of Christ. Love is creative only when it is passionate. Great passions are dangerous and often become excessive—especially when devoted to a mean and mediocre object. But good psychologists today agree with Pascal that it is better to repair the damage done by excess than to eliminate passion altogether. Kierkegaard was certainly right when he said that the man who has lost all in passionate love has lost less than the man who has never known it.

The Fear of Passion

The more mature and alive a man is the more passionately he lives and loves. People who are immature cannot cope with passion. They suffer from aversions, but never from moral indignation. They satisfy and pool their needs but are incapable of the vehement passion of love. They are forced to rely on law, routine, custom, whim, or rational calculation.

Most of us are so terribly afraid of passion precisely because it leads us beyond the measured boundaries of the conscious self, the superficial ego. Our fear leads us to settle for some convenient and comfortable substitutions. If we cannot control passion in the neatly systematic way we handle everything else in our technological world, we skip it altogether.

There are a million ways of letting the flesh snuff out the life of the spirit. But the popular, canonized American way that seems to include most if not all of the others is our compulsive pursuit of happiness. The notion of happiness as a birthright was not original with Thomas Jefferson; it was a dominant theme of both the French Revolution and the Age of Enlightenment,

Americanized by Jefferson. It would be a remarkable feat to expunge from our American psyches our high expectations of happiness. "The only orthodox object of the institution of government," according to Jefferson, "is to secure the greatest degree of happiness possible to the general masses of those associated under it." What this highly vaunted happiness—the American achievement—finally came to mean was simply "not being pained in body or troubled in mind."

Keep that lifeless, passionless definition in mind while you reexamine our political and social institutions, our military-industrial complex, our technology, hospitals, schools, our churches, and our families. Are they making us whole—that is, holy: "Be perfect as your heavenly Father is perfect" (Mt. 5:48)—or are they merely making us happy?

Happiness is a big business these days. We will do anything to be happy: tell lies, cheat, break international alliances, matrimonial bonds, pledges of friendship and love, as well as religious commitments. We will dismiss our old people and kill our unborn infants. We thrash around in and out of war and in and out of each other's beds, pursuing the shadow of our happiness.

Ultimately we refuse to live because there is no way to live without suffering. Passion (*passio*) literally means the suffering of life, creatively, gloriously. To refuse to suffer or to spend a lifetime trying to avoid it, is to refuse to live, to love, to be. Our American preoccupation with happiness turns out to be a deathwish.

In the December 1974 issue of *Esquire* Malcolm Muggeridge wrote a biting, stinging piece on this disgraceful and ironic state of affairs in America and entitled his article "The Decade of the Great Liberal Death Wish." It is worth quoting at some length as a way of summing up and clarifying in magnificent Muggeridgean fashion how our rabid pursuit of happiness has left us half alive:

> I have a recurrent nightmare that somehow or other a lot of contemporary pabulum—video tape of television programs with accompanying advertisements, news footage, copies of newspapers and magazines, stereo tapes of pop groups and other cacophonies, best-selling novels, films and other such material—gets preserved like the Dead Sea Scrolls, in some

remote salt cave. Then some centuries, or maybe millennia, later, when our civilization will long since have joined all others that once were and now can only be patiently reconstructed out of dusty ruins, incomprehensible hieroglyphics and other residuary relics, archaeologists discover the cave, and set out sorting out its contents and trying to deduce from them what we were like and how we lived. (That is assuming, of course, that we do not, in the process of working out the great liberal death wish, blow ourselves and our earth to smithereens—a large assumption.) What will they make of us? I wonder. Materially, so rich and so powerful; spiritually, so impoverished and fear-ridden. Having made such remarkable inroads into the secrets of nature; beginning to explore, and perhaps to colonize, the universe itself; developing the means to produce in more or less unlimited quantities everything we could possibly need or desire, and to transmit swifter than light every thought, smile, or word that could possibly delight, entertain or instruct us. Disposing of treasure beyond calculation, opening up possibilities beyond conception. Yet haunted and obsessed by the fear that we are too numerous; that soon as our numbers go on increasing there will be no room or food for us. On the one hand, a neurotic passion to increase consumption, sustained by every sort of imbecile persuasion; on the other, ever-increasing hunger and penury among the so-called backward or underdeveloped peoples. Never, our archaeologists will surely conclude, was any generation of men intent upon the pursuit of happiness more advantageously placed to attain it, who yet with seeming deliberation, took the opposite course—toward chaos, not order; toward breakdown, not stability; toward death, destruction and darkness, not life, creativity and light. An ascent that ran downhill; plenty that turned into a wasteland; a cornucopia whose abundance made hungry; a death wish inexorably unfolding.[3]

To suppress a death wish it is necessary to proclaim a corresponding life wish, as Jesus did with "the Good News," to will one thing: eternal life. "And this is eternal life, that you may know God and Jesus Christ whom he has sent" (Jn. 17:3).

---

3. Malcolm Muggeridge, "The Decade of the Great Liberal Death Wish," *Esquire*, December 1974, p. 156.

The Good News involves the existential knowledge of being loved by God, of sharing Christ's own experience of that love. What we *do* must be an unmistakable witness of that *loving awareness*.

But so many of the things we do have nothing to do with be-ingfulness and, therefore, nothing to do with the loving will of God. These feverish activities of ours are then happy and haughty distractions. If we don't have the insight and the inscape to do better, then we inevitably succumb to the tyranny of diversion; we become do-gooders in a frenzied effort to compensate for our passion deficiency. We mollify our stricken consciences by plunging into a plethora of prodigious doings, but we almost cease to be. Thus we are duped, deluded, and driven, and consequently lose our grip on life.

Because of the compulsiveness of our urban preoccupations we do not hear the Word of God; we do not sense the urgency of the Son, the Shepherd, rescuing us and bringing us back home. This deafness (the English for *absurdus*) equals absurdity. Is it any wonder then that absurdity characterizes our age?

The compulsion to do good prevents us from ever becoming good. God alone is good, all good because he knows how *to be*, simply and unfailingly. His own burning passion is to let us be; and our own human goal, our finest and final aspiration, is to be—fully, exuberantly, divinely. That is when we become good as well as conspicuously and contagiously alive: when Being engulfs us. That's when we let God be God. And that's when, with passionate passivity, we allow the Son of God to shepherd us into Being.

Dedicated as we are to the pursuit of our own happiness or the happiness of others, we are bound to be hypocritical. Hypocrisy is the great enemy of the spirit, of man at his truest and best. It grows like lichen on high ideals because it can become a personal protection from the demands of the spirit by substituting for them others which belong only to the Law. Legalism and formalism are types of hypocrisy. So is sentimental morality which uses the form of law, custom, and ritual, not as a support for spirit but as a substitute. By using the external organization of the community (the Law), hypocrisy imposes false standards which claim to be spiritual. Crass authorities consolidate power in the flesh by demanding obedience as due in the spirit. The "letter kills the spirit" (2 Cor. 3:6). This enormous devotion to the "letter," to "the way things are," to the enclosed world of the flesh, is the unforgivable sin against the Spirit. "Woe to you, Scribes and Pharisees, hypocrites! For you are like whitewashed tombs, which outwardly appear beautiful, but within they are full of dead men's bones, and all uncleanness" (Mt. 23:27).

As harsh as he was toward the Scribes and the Pharisees, Christ did not come to destroy the Law, but to fulfill it. There is to the Law a necessary and proper function. But it still is merely a condition of something infinitely higher. Christ loved and valued it insofar as it served the life of the spirit and the realm of truth. The Law works if it establishes a climate of enlightened openness in which deep love relationships can prosper, not only horizontally, but vertically.

Jesus came to stir up the life of the spirit, to abolish all the barriers to a unifying love. But his revolutionary ideas were interpreted according to the Law which prevailed at his time. His new concept of freedom could take root but not possibly fully develop at that time. Christ planted the seed. St. Paul altered the whole moral balance, introducing a new criterion of morality, illumined love instead of Law. But the Christian trend was not strong enough to break through the embedded rigidity of the Roman Empire. Christ came to free us. Are we ready now to become free?

Most of us are not. We choose the well-worn pathways and follow the crowd. We join the wrong communities and marry the wrong people—like Henry Crawford in Jane Austen's *Mansfield Park*.

Henry's passion for Fanny could not break down the strong defenses of his vanity and selfishness. He eloped with Maria whom he despised. His subsequent vexation was not the sorrow of repentance that leads to the possibility of new love, but a self-justifying anger. John Updike's recent play on President Buchanan reveals a similar method for evading the devastating demands of a passionate life according to the spirit. In act one young Buchanan is engaged to marry Anne Coleman. But he is unable to face the unreasonable realm that passionate love would open up to him. He subtly rejects the girl, who then kills herself. Act two presents

Buchanan's last months as president. Unable to respond to the unreasoned passions of the South, he again copes with the caution and legalism which protected him from Anne's ardor.

Oddly enough, like Buchanan, we succeed in being moderately happy: by finding the most apathetic slot from which we participate in life guardedly, if at all. Apathy is a withdrawal of feeling—*a-pathos* or passionlessness. It is not the most spectacular form of suicide, but it is the most common. It has been eroding our civilization for a century and more and is about to reach its apogee, and all in the name of progress and the pursuit of happiness. Without passion, apathy is inevitable or, at best, a complacent mediocrity. When a community or a nation needs to be recreated and invested with verve, administrators and statesmen should be replaced by passionate leaders.

The Flight from Eros into Sex

Sex, sought with avid abandon, is the key to the pursuit of happiness. Sex is the powerful production and release of bodily tensions. Eros, in contrast, is the power which deeply personalizes the purpose and significantly grasps the meaning of the act.

Eros, which is the Greek word for passion, is not synonymous with sexual titillation or what we commonly refer to as "eroticism." The Greeks emphasized eros; that is why that Greek word is so familiar to us. They deemphasized sex; that is why we hardly know what term they used for it. Eros pertains essentially to the art of making love (*coming into union*—communion). Sex is limited to the manipulation of organs. Eros attracts and lures us into union with everything. Eros is wakeful, vigilant, remembering whatever is true and beautiful, whatever is good. Sex is a need; eros is a desire. The sex act is, indeed, the most potent symbolic and specific celebration of relatedness imaginable. But eros *is* relatedness. Excitement accompanies sex. Tenderness dominates the erotic quest.

Eros is the longing to enjoy such deep and wide-ranged dimensions of relatedness—all originating from a critical center and tending toward an ultimate end—that a unitive and beautifying fruition of Being is experienced, at least incipiently and intermittently, on this earth. Although dramatically and supremely important in a good sexual relationship, the same erotic desire for union plays a central part in man's rapport with animal and plant life, as well as with aesthetic, philosophical, ethical, scientific, socio-political, and religious forms. Eros relates us not only to other persons whom we love, but to the pig we are raising, the house we are building, the car we are driving, the vocation we are following. If we had been sufficiently charged with eros, for instance, we would have participated in a reverent dialogue with our environment which would have precluded the ecological disaster we are now suffering—the catastrophic conditions of our natural world brought on by the petty passions of uninspired and unconcerned hordes of hollow men.

Eros urges us to be united with the beloved, to prolong delight, to discover deeper dimensions of love's meaning and to treasure the memory of being together. As Rollo May points out, the most memorable moment of sexual love-making is not the final orgasm, but the penetrating entrance into the secret caverns of the body-person. Apocalypse, however, is not between a woman's legs. But that incomparably beautiful arch may be the gateway into the transcendent mystery of the universe. Notice how often photographers try to capture the indescribable splendor of a woman with legs spread magnificently apart in a stately stance of irresistible appeal or a graceful stride across an open space. Far from cheap or even sexy, this photography strives to capture an artistic and transsexual symbol of the incarnational structure of human existence. Through that feminine archway man discovers his own *anima*, the feminine principle within his own being, and realizes simultaneously, if he is fully aware and in tune, that the apocalyptic paradise for which he yearns and toward which the whole universe is spinning, may lie through that gorgeous portal, but infinitely beyond. Woman elevates the *reverent* man. Eros urges man to transcend himself, soaring into realms of the spirit through symbols of the flesh.

The singlehearted, great-souled thrust of eros, the yearning for wholeness, gives form, vitality, and unity to our lives. If I do not reduce my passion to lust—and that is every man's temptation—then I shall enjoy what the Greeks called a pregnant soul. In other words, I shall be a creator, an inventor, an artist, collaborating in some little way with the Spirit in the building up of God's Kingdom in the world.

Highly cultivated, eros will empower me to understand that there is no such thing as a separate creature or an isolated event. If I am erotic enough I will see the connection, the binding element in the universe, the interactive process of being and becoming.

"Eros is the center of the vitality of a culture—its heart and soul," wrote Rollo May. "And when release of tension takes the place of creative eros, the downfall of the civilization is assured."[4] Along with Rollo May I lament the death of eros in our age. When there is no erotic vitality at the center of a person or a culture, decadence sets in. When the release of tension replaces creatively mounting passion, the degradation of man and the collapse of his civilization is assured.

Sex seems to be an outstanding way for a moribund society of robots to prove that they have some live animality left in them. David Riesman in *The Lonely Crowd* calls it the "last frontier." Gerald Sykes, in *The Cool Millennium*, remarks: "In a world gone grey with market reports, time studies, tax regulations and path lab analyses, the rebel finds sex to be the one green thing."

But without the fire of eros the frontier freshness of sex didn't last long. We have ended up fussing interminably with research and statistics. We have reduced love to sex, sex to genitality, and genitality to technique.

Fearful of the dangerous, driving force of eros, we have turned this deep source of love and life into manageable and measurable sex. Promoters of packaged passion like Hugh Heffner and Dr. Alex Comfort keep our society pleasant but respectable by distributing a carefully calculated measure of sexual "kicks."

The world is full of pepless playboys but bereft of passionate lovers. While passionate feeling has decreased, coital technique has increased and has prepared the way for one of the monstrosities of modern man: casual copulation. People today would rather be competent performers of cool sex than raptured contemplatives,

---

4. Rollo May, *Love and Will* (New York: Dell Publishing Co., 1969), p. 98.

surprised by joy and lifted beyond their control into olympian orbits of ecstasy. Passion is repressed for the sake of performance; sensuality is mistaken for sensitivity. Is it really a liberating leap in sexual style if our technical prowess, with easy access in and out of coition, inhibits our feelings and suffocates our passion?

There is no sexual revolution, only a copulation explosion. The new sexual "freedom" allows us to perform profusely, which generally means frequently, quickly, and lovelessly. Our flight from eros embarrasses and frustrates us. We attempt to cover our shame with sexual activities of high frequency and low value. Our exploits are flimsy, compulsive and unrelated to love. The wild and wonderful passion of eros has been replaced by the timid sensation of sex. Having repressed passion and stifled love, we have nothing sexual left to celebrate except technique.

Technique promises us everything instantly: virtue without effort, knowledge without discipline, love without knowledge, intimacy without love, wisdom without struggle, peace without pain, style without formation, sex without risk, success without trying—provided that we settle for a passionless existence. The religious quest is dominated by the same trend: Christianity without religion, mysticism without asceticism, prayer without passion (nirvana), union without persons (Oriental bliss).

According to Rollo May:

> . . . there comes a point (and this is the challenge facing modern technological Western man) when the cult of technique destroys feeling, undermines passion, and blots out individual identity. The technologically efficient lover, defeated in the contradiction which is copulation without eros, is ultimately the impotent one. He has lost the power to be carried away; he knows only too well what he is doing. At this point, technology diminishes consciousness and demolishes eros. Tools are no longer an enlargement of consciousness but a substitute for it, and indeed, tend to repress and truncate it.[5]

This management of mystery forces us to skim the surface of life deprived of significance and sanctity.

---

5. *Ibid.*, pp. 97-98.

Tragedy and Fidelity

We have reduced eros to sex because we are afraid to love; and we are afraid to love because love leads to death. Love hungers to be with the beloved other, to become the beloved other. This kind of presence and union only come about through ego-reduction resulting in ego-death. Once I have reduced egotistic craving to zero I am free to be with and to become the beloved other. Until then, I am trapped within the confines of the isolated ego.

The coital act is a sexual symbolic celebration of love and a psycho-physical symbol of death. In any act of genuine intercourse, the lover dies to self, and rises not only in the life of the beloved, but in the life of the entirely new entity of two become one. Our preoccupation with sexual prowess distracts us from that awful death which lies at the heart of every love-act. Our deliriously frequent couplings disguise a lifelessness which is the inevitable consequence of deathlessness in our sex as well as every other dimension of our lives. The Victorian Age repressed sex. We use sex itself to repress the nearness, necessity, and inevitability of death.

Erotic love, of course, hurls me into heights and depths simultaneously. In other words, my life is bound to be tragic. But what right has a professional lover of the world, a Christ-man, to expect anything but a tragic life? Tragedy is not catastrophe. It is what happens to human lives that burst the bounds of rational control and the norms of conventional standards. Think of the great love stories, mythic or historical: Helen and Paris, Tristan and Isolde, Cathy and Heathcliff, Abelard and Heloise, Romeo and Juliet. The life of Christ is the best example.

Love-force or soul-power is a tragic gift. It can devastate a man like a landslide so that he can never rise again to the heights of God. But even such a tragic figure is closer to sanctity—and to God—than the exemplary citizen who cannot even understand the dangers to which the other has succumbed, who knows nothing of that stormy upward sweep of his soul, the self-expenditure involved in the suffering of life, with a whole heart rendered and sundered. There is no love without tragedy, only insipid substitutions. The only tragedy that is really catastrophe is the death of love. A broken vow, a collapsed friendship, a love betrayed, a cherished secret divulged are worse than the destruction of the Golden Gate Bridge.

Our greatest erotic responsibility is to keep love alive. It isn't easy. What happens when passion breaks through? A hidden force breaks through the protective and necessary layers of custom and habitual ways of thought and behavior and pushes back the assumed boundaries of the up-to-now stuck-in-the-mud self. After a while the ravages of time take their toll. The original emotion slackens. The original impetus wanes, although the value is still prized.

At this point the tendency of the flesh is to resume "business as usual" and return to "normal." The really passionate person will prevent this regression by freely and deliberately choosing appropriate human activities that will continue to relate him significantly to the same value and all that it progressively stands for, even when the original emotion connected with the value has faded.

Rosemary Haughton points out that pure passion must, if it is not to degenerate, renew itself by contact with its source, by means of action related to the symbol which gave it birth.[6] This is the function of sex in marriage and of the Eucharist in the Christian community. As the life of the Spirit increases it can depend less on the power of the symbol; for instance, a devoted elderly couple depend less on sexual attraction and genitality; a spiritually mature person depends less on Eucharistic celebrations. Both sex and Eucharist remain important, but not in the same way.

Falling in love may be romance, but staying in love is mysticism. Romantic love is a good beginning but a poor end. It takes persistent passion to turn romantic sentiment or esthetic taste into a stubborn and seasoned mystical love. Only mystical love can make sense out of the indissolubility of the marriage bond or the permanency of a celibate vow.

In mystical love there is always something going on—a deeper exploration into the truth, the inscrutable *thouness* of the beloved, and therefore an unflagging loyalty to his uniqueness in

---

6. Rosemary Haughton, *On Trying to be Human* (Springfield, Ill.: Templegate, 1966).

whom God is revealed as in no other. If divine revelation is finished, then the lovers are finished. Only thus does God become supremely important; and if he is not supremely important he is not important at all. Only if a man and woman's relationship is supremely important will they remain faithful.

We have not grasped the ultimate seriousness and sacredness of a single human act because we have not understood how absolutely unique every human being really is. To be unique is not a matter of peculiar differences but of outstanding fidelity. When all is said and done that is what the spiritual life is all about, *fidelity*: to myself and the God who calls me to become more and more gracefully myself, my very best self; not in isolation but in communion with the whole human race. My passion must go on mounting until I am so faithful that God will look on me with pleasure and say: "This is my beloved son" (Mt. 3:17).

At the close of the *Purgatorio*, Beatrice says to Dante: "You should have been faithful to my beloved flesh," and in her eyes he actually sees reflected the two-natured Gryphon of Christ. The only way to be faithful to the flesh is by the quickened penetration and transformation of the flesh by the ardor of the Spirit of Christ. No puny passions will do, but the total thrust of our erotic being toward the Absolutely Loving God, and therefore toward full participation in the Christlife on earth. This faithful following of Christ into the All, and this alone, will make each of us unique and empower us to respond uniquely and wholeheartedly to every unique situation.

This was the genius of Christ! And the gist of Christianity at its best. This is the earthly destiny of every person: to be so alive, so completely awakened, that he moves in and out of concrete human exigencies at a passionate pitch of loving awareness.

> I am a bow in your hands, Lord.
> Draw me, lest I rot.
>
> Do not overdraw me, Lord. I shall break.
>
> Overdraw me, Lord, and who cares if I break?[7]

---

7. Nikos Kazantzakis, *Report to Greco* (New York: Simon and Schuster, 1965), frontispiece.

Eros – OT
passion – pp 33-34 & p 108 & p 114

are of God's name pp 64-65   POWERFUL

love – pp 68-69

Lent – p 96-97

shell of a man   p 109
    (passionless)
authentic self (sex)   p 110

eros
quest   ⟩ passion ⟩ agape
symbols & signs   love
                              God